Dear Friend,

I am pleased to send you this copy of Robert J. Morgan's *100 Bible Verses Everyone Should Know by Heart*. Robert credits my mother with teaching him how to pray God's Word and encouraging him to memorize Scripture while he was a student at Montreat College.

Memorizing God's Word is a powerful tool for living the Christian life. Pointing to benefits such as "clearer thoughts, steadier nerves, healthier emotions, purer habits, happier homes, greater respect, [and] eternal optimism," Robert gives us compelling reasons for committing Scripture to memory and offers tools to help us do it. I pray that this book will both challenge and equip you to "hide God's word in your heart" (see Psalm 119:11) and, as a result, experience His presence in a new and deeper way.

For more than 60 years, the Billy Graham Evangelistic Association has worked to take the Good News of Jesus Christ throughout the world by every effective means available, and I'm excited about what God will do in the years ahead.

We would appreciate knowing how this ministry has touched your life. May God richly bless you.

Sincerely,

Franklin Graham
President

If you would like to know more, please contact us:

IN THE U.S.:
Billy Graham Evangelistic Association
1 Billy Graham Parkway
Charlotte, NC 28201-0001
billygraham.org
info@bgea.org
Toll-free: 1-877-247-2426

IN CANADA:
Billy Graham Evangelistic
Association of Canada
20 Hopewell Way NE
Calgary, AB T3J 5H5
billygraham.ca
Toll-free: 1-888-393-0003

100
BIBLE
VERSES

everyone should know by heart

This *Billy Graham Library Selection* is published with permission from B&H Publishing Group.

PUBLISHING GROUP

©2010 by Robert J. Morgan
All rights reserved.
Printed in the United States of America

ISBN 978-1-59328-326-1
Previous 978-0-8054-4682-1

Published by B&H Publishing Group
Nashville, Tennessee

Dewey Decimal Classification: 220.07
Subject Heading: BIBLE—STUDY AND TEACHING \
BIBLE—MEMORIZING \ CHRISTIAN LIFE

In Bible verses at times the author italicizes words for emphasis.

9 10 11 12 13 • 15 14 13 12 11

To
Ava Grace

CONTENTS

Listening: The Word of God and Prayer

Assurance: Inner Peace and Security

Praise: Worship and Thanksgiving

Promises: Verses to Stand On

Holiness: Obeying God's Commands

Fullness: The Holy Spirit's Role in Our Lives

Joy: God's Kind of Happiness

Alpha and Omega: The First and Second Comings of Christ

100 WAYS TO CHANGE YOUR LIFE

This book is about the archaic custom of memorizing Scripture, why we must revive it, and how you can begin a lifelong habit of learning Bible verses by heart. Think of it as a shopping spree for the mind, a chance to collect and store up treasures you'll enjoy for years.

Restoring the art of Scripture memory is crucial for us, our churches, and children. It's vital for mental and emotional health and for spiritual well-being. Though it's as easy as repeating words aloud, it's as powerful as acorns dropping into furrows in the forest. It makes the Bible portable; you can take it with you everywhere without packing it in purse or briefcase. It makes Scripture accessible day and night. It allows God's Word to sink into your brain and permeate your subconscious and even your unconscious thoughts. It gives you a word to say to anyone, in season and out of season. It fills your heart and home with the best thoughts ever recorded. It saturates the personality, satiates the soul, and stockpiles the mind. It changes the atmosphere of every family and alters the weather forecast of every day.

It takes one minute a day, or five or ten—whatever you can devote to it. It can be done in your bath, your bed, at your desk, or in an airplane (you can't say all that about too many things). It can be done on the go, in traffic jams, while shaving, at sunup, or before bedtime. It can be done alone, with another person, or in groups. It's an amazingly versatile habit but also a vital one, profitable whether we're in the nursery or in the nursing home.

Here, then, are 100 ways to change your life—100 Bible verses everyone on earth should know by heart. Please don't complain if your favorite verse isn't among them. I kept changing my list even up to publication date; but I've left a blank page in the back so you can add your own verses and keep the habit going.

I'm deeply grateful to my literary partners: Thomas Walters, my editor; Chris Ferebee, my agent; Sherry Anderson and Emily Youree, my assistants; my Web expert and advisor, Joshua Rowe; and my dear wife, Katrina, who read every word with a keen eye. Undying thanks also goes to the church I've had the joy of pastoring for thirty years— The Donelson Fellowship of Nashville—who participated in a yearlong sermon series on which this book is based.

If you'd like to contact me, please visit my Web site at www.robertjmorgan.com, where you'll also find free supplemental resources, including a study guide, publicity tools, and downloadable materials for churches and small groups wanting to learn these 100 verses together.

PART ONE

THE POWER
OF SCRIPTURE MEMORY

For as he thinks within himself, so he is.

(Proverbs 23:7 NASB)

ONE

AS WE THINK

James Allen has been called a literary man of mystery. Little is known about him, and his writing career was as fleeting as an arrow through the sky. He never achieved fame or fortune, and he died at forty-eight. He wrote nineteen or twenty books without saying much about himself in any of them; and none of them sold particularly well in his lifetime. Yet one tiny volume—his second book and one with which he himself was unhappy—has since sold millions of copies and influenced countless lives.

James was born in 1864, in an idyllic part of central England; but his childhood wasn't so idyllic. His father, grappling with a failing business and near bankruptcy, traveled to America, searching for a new job. Instead, he was waylaid, robbed, and murdered. Back in England, the family's ensuing financial crisis forced young James to drop out of school at age fifteen and get a job. He became a personal assistant in the world of British manufacturers, and he worked at that profession until 1902, when, at age thirty-eight, he just quit and walked away.

James and his wife moved to the little coastal town of Ilfracombe, one of the loveliest spots in all England, and he lived there for about ten years before his early death. He kept a strict routine. Each morning he'd get up before dawn and hike to the top of the nearby hillside and spend an hour in meditation. Then he would return to his house and devote the morning to writing. The afternoons he allocated to his gardens and hobbies.

To the best of my knowledge, he was not a Christian, but one little book was based on a Bible verse from the book of Proverbs, and that small volume has cast a long shadow. It almost single-handedly gave rise to the self-improvement and positive thinking movement of the past 100 years.

It's entitled *As a Man Thinketh,* based on Proverbs 23:7: "For as he thinks in his heart, so is he" (NKJV). The point of *As a Man Thinketh* is simple: Our thoughts are the most important thing about us. All that we achieve or fail to achieve is the direct result of our thinking. Our thoughts are like seeds that produce crops.

Allen wrote: "Good thoughts and actions can never produce bad results; bad thoughts and actions can never produce good results. This is but saying that nothing can come from corn but corn, nothing from nettles but nettles. Men understand this law in the natural world, and work with it; but few understand it in the mental and moral world (though its operation there is just as simple and undeviating)."[1]

His point is that we *are* what we *think*, and our lives run in the direction of our thoughts. If we think angry thoughts, we'll be angry; if we think positive thoughts, we'll be positive; if we think negative thoughts, we'll be negative. The mind is a garden, and we have to cultivate it, and we are responsible for the kind of seed we sow into the furrows of our mind.

To quote Allen again: "A [person's] mind may be likened to a garden, which may be intelligently cultivated or allowed to run wild; but whether cultivated or neglected, it must, and will, bring forth. If no useful seeds are put into it, then an abundance of useless seeds will fall therein, and will continue to produce their kind."[2]

I love Allen's little book, and I believe in positive thinking, optimism, and a can-do spirit. But I'm not a fan of most of the positive-thinking literature so popular in the self-help sections of our bookstores. I want *Truth* behind my optimism—solid Scripture, well interpreted. I don't want a mind filled with mottoes and mantras but with memory verses from the infallible Word of God.

I believe the Bible is the inspired and unfailing message from a God who is both intimate and infinite, and who is omniscient and omnipotent. It verbalizes His revealed intelligence about how we should think, feel, act, and speak. Its theology is therapeutic, and its advice is sensible. Every verse in the Bible is priceless, for all Scripture is given by inspiration of God; and we're to live by every word that proceeds from the mouth of God (2 Tim. 3:16; Matt. 4:4).

As a parent and a pastor, I've tried for decades to drop the seeds of specific Scriptures into the furrows of my thoughts—and into the minds of others. Scripture memory is a way of digging into the soul and planting the truth a little deeper in order to achieve a richer harvest. Yes, it's a lost habit among most people; but losing it is like an explorer losing his map or a nation losing her constitution.

In the following pages let me show you what Scripture memory can do for you and how you can develop this enriching routine. A verse learned goes into our memories and from there into our conscious and subconscious minds. From there it appears in the room of imagination, from whence it shows up in the way we live, think, feel, talk, act, and achieve. The principle of Proverbs 23:7 is true 24-7. It is an inviolable law of life that cannot be altered and will be true as long as human nature endures: For as we think in our hearts so are we.

Precept upon precept, line upon line. . .
Here a little, there a little.

(Isaiah 28:13 NKJV)

TWO

GETTING SCRIPTURE INTO THE MEMORY

You'll never guess where I began learning the scores—hundreds, really—of Bible verses that have filled my mind for about a half century. It was at Eastside Elementary School in Elizabethton, Tennessee. This small redbrick schoolhouse was two blocks from my house, and I spent six happy years of my life there. Thankfully the prohibition against Bible reading in public schools hadn't yet taken effect in my little town. I remember hearing about the Supreme Court decision in 1963 that outlawed prayer and Bible reading in public classrooms. I was eleven years old, but I recall how shocked everyone seemed at this discrimination against Christians.

But that didn't stop us from memorizing Bible verses, aided by an intrepid gentleman who came once a week from the Children's Bible Mission. When I was in the first grade, I memorized John 3:16 and received a lovely little wall plaque as a reward. In the second grade I learned the entire Twenty-third Psalm and was given a small New Testament. In the third grade I learned twenty-five more verses, and I've forgotten what the reward was for that; it might have been a Bible containing both Old and New Testaments. In the fourth grade it was fifty verses, and in the fifth and sixth grades we were presented with a challenging 100 verses per year, and if we learned all 100, we were given a free week at summer camp.

The incentives have long since perished, but many of these verses have stayed with me for a lifetime. Through the years I've consistently added to their stockpile. These verses have resourced my mentality. They have kept me from making many mistakes, from losing my temper on multiple occasions, and from committing sins that would have marred my soul. They've given me encouragement during challenging moments, comfort during grief, peace amid alarm, and joy when the sun was obscured by clouds of confusion.

These verses have also given me something to say to others on many occasions when my own words were uncertain or inadequate. Scripture has power that is supernatural, soothing, convicting, transforming, life-changing, timely, timeless, and eternal. Nothing beats having the Word of God stored away in the chambers of the mind.

I'm finding it harder now to commit new verses to memory—our memorizers slow down as we grow older—but I'm still working on it.

My view is this: If it's good for an elementary classroom in a mountain school in Tennessee, it's good enough for a philosophy classroom at the University of California in Los Angeles.

Not long ago I had an interesting chat with Dallas Willard about memorizing Scripture. Dr. Willard is a professor in the School of Philosophy at UCLA and an outstanding thinker and writer. He's also a keen advocate of Scripture memory. I asked him why he felt so strongly about it, and he told me that his life was shaped, in large part, by growing up in an environment that stressed engraving God's Word on the furrows of the heart.

"I've found that through Scripture memory the incredible treasures of Scripture are not only just available to my mind, but they inform my whole being in a way that is a testimony to the substantial power of the Word of God," he said.

Dr. Willard suggests memorizing whole passages instead of isolated verses, and I agree.

"Memorizing miscellaneous verses is a good thing, but when I talk about memorizing Scripture, I'm really talking about memorizing passages, whole Psalms, or long parts of the Letters or the Gospels," said Willard. "That does something to not only your mind but to your outlook. For me, anything that is going to be effective in spiritual formation or growth in grace has got to be holistic. It can't be a little side thing that you have a few Scriptures memorized. A simple illustration is the Twenty-third Psalm. Many people have that memorized, but they don't allow it to inform their thinking and their acting by meditating on it as they should. Having it stored in your mind is a powerful resource for inner development."

He added, "It's also important for (sharing with others) because it's strange how having long passages of the Word of God inscribed in your mind just brings outlines, insights, and ways of putting things that will inform your speaking, your conversation, and your preaching. That's the main thing I have found out by use, that there's power in long passages of the Word being committed to memory."[3]

Dr. Willard is right. When we layer one verse upon another, working our way through passages and memorizing Scripture contextually, we're more likely to interpret it accurately through the process of meditation. So consider the book you're holding in your hands a tool for locating 100 different passages to delve into, not just 100 miscellaneous verses.

But the great thing about Scripture memory is you can learn long passages in small steps—one word at a time, one verse after another. You don't have to start with a long passage or even with a long verse. Just start with one word—the first word of the verse, then add the next, and the next.

As Isaiah put it, "Precept upon precept; . . . line upon line; here a little, and there a little (Isa. 28:13 KJV). It's like painting the inside of your mind with God's colors, one brushstroke at a time.

THREE

GETTING SCRIPTURE INTO THE SUBCONSCIOUS

Philip Turner, small-town attorney, realized he was waking up in the intensive care unit of a hospital somewhere, for reasons he couldn't fathom. There were machines and strange blinking lights and sounds. His body didn't feel right, and concerned faces hovered above him. He closed his eyes and tried to think. He listened to the electronic hums of a strange and sterile place, the *beep beep beep* of a machine he'd rather not have heard so close to his ear.

It had been a balmy evening in Shelbyville, Illinois, and a friend had dropped by Philip's house, suggesting a nocturnal plane ride. Philip and his wife, Bobbie, were game. They drove out to the town's small airstrip, climbed into a four-seater Beech Musketeer, and a few minutes later were airborne, looking down on their serene, sleeping town, recognizing landmarks, and feeling like birds soaring through the moonlit darkness.

A few minutes later the runway lights came into view, and the passengers prepared for landing.

That's the last thing Philip remembered. Later he learned that the nose wheel of the Musketeer hit a power line, flipping the plane over. Bobbie was thrown through the side window onto the ground while Philip remained suspended, head downward, in his seat belt with over a hundred fractures.

As he regained consciousness, Philip's mind was fragmented with scattered, confused images. Hours passed, and as his head began to clear, a series of thoughts suddenly came into his mind like brilliant shafts of light. *Not that we loved God, but that He loved us. . . . Who hath saved us, not according to our works, but according to His own purpose and grace. . . . Fear not. . . . For God so loved the world. . . . Is there anything too hard for me?*

These were fragments of Bible verses, but Philip wasn't a religious man, and he didn't go to church. He hadn't opened a Bible in years, and he had certainly never memorized any Bible verses.

Or had he? Slowly a few vague memories filtered into his mind. A little circle of red chairs. Old Mrs. Wolf with an open Bible on her lap. Little cards. Awards.

As a five-year-old boy, Philip had attended a Sunday school class, and the teacher had drilled them on Bible verses. Those who learned the verses were given prizes, but Philip had never earned any awards; he had been a disappointment to Mrs. Wolf. Yet down in the depths of his brain, those memory verses lay like dormant seeds, waiting for just the right moment to germinate.

Philip and Bobbie slowly recovered from their injuries, and in the process they committed themselves to Christ and started going to church. Many years later, as he recounted the story to me over the phone, he was enthusiastic about memorizing Scripture and about the need to plant Bible verses in the minds of youngsters of all ages. His life had been changed by verses he did not even remember having learned.

Some people question the value of rote memory, and I'll admit that just memorizing words for the sake of words is of limited value. But Bible verses are not just words. We may not fully understand every verse we memorize, but the act of learning it pins it to our short-term memories. From our short-term memory, it filters into our long-term brain cells. It sinks into our subconscious minds, and as time passes the results can be dramatic.

And always dramatically good.

That's what I learned while listening to Mr. Turner tell me about the little circle of red chairs, about an old woman with an open Bible in her lap, and about the power of memorizing the most potent words in the universe—the verses found within the covers of the inspired Word of God.[4]

When we memorize a word, phrase, line, or verse from God's Word, it's like implanting a powerful radioactive speck of the very mind of God into our own finite brains. As we review it or hear it spoken again, it sinks deeper into our heads. As we learn it "by heart," it descends into the hidden crevices and fissures of our souls. As we meditate on it, it begins sending out its quiet, therapeutic waves of influence. And, as the apostle Paul said, we are transformed by the renewing of our thoughts (see Rom. 12:2).

That's why the Lord commands us in Proverbs 7:1, 3: "Treasure my commands. . . . Write them on the tablet of your heart."

And that's why He promises in the first psalm that as we internalize His Word and mull over it day and night, we'll be successful, converting *His logic* into *our lives*. We'll be like apple trees planted by rivers of water, bearing fruit in season, with leaves that don't wither; and whatever we do will prosper.

FOUR

GETTING SCRIPTURE INTO THE IMAGINATION

For those needing a little extra courage to take the plunge into Scripture memory (or into any other endeavor), consider our granddaughter, Chloe, age nine. Here's an e-mail our daughter Victoria sent to us last night about their outing to the YMCA. With our son-in-law Ethan in Iraq with U.S. forces, Victoria and her seven girls have taken advantage of a free membership our local YMCA gives military families. This week they've gone swimming in the evenings.

Victoria wrote, "We ate pizza for supper and went to the Y. It was a good way to end the week. On Tuesday the oldest four, with the exception of Chloe, took the swimming test so they could go into the deep end. Chloe struggled and struggled in the shallow end with me. She finally came over to me and said, 'Mom, I'm disappointed in myself that I don't have enough faith in myself to try.'

"So I told her three things: (1) that even if she never takes the plunge, she is just as special, and I love her just as much as if she passes a thousand swimming tests; (2) that she should use her mind and imagine herself doing it over and over until she believes it; (3) that the Lord is the One who helps us conquer fears because He is bigger and stronger and He gives us strength on the inside.

"She mulled all of it over and never took the test. Later that evening she told me she was imagining herself doing the swimming test. She struggled all night with this inner battle, and I just had to let her. There wasn't anything I could do except let her struggle through the process.

"Tonight we had only been at the pool about ten minutes, and she came over to me and told me she was taking it and marched right to the lifeguard and told him. She swam from the deep end to the shallow end beautifully. I quickly had to wipe my tears so she didn't see me cry. I don't think I've ever been prouder of her. That's my girl!"

I think Victoria's advice will work in any pool we're in. We tap into a powerful force whenever we combine prayer, imagination, and initiative. Most professional athletes now have mental coaches who help them train through visualization, and I've read about Olympians who were sidelined by injuries yet ended up winning the gold or silver because they continued training in their minds when they couldn't do so with their bodies. One diver visualized every second of her routine day after day, using intense, focused concentration. She recovered from the disabled list just in time for the games, and she ended up on the winner's platform.

Just last week I finished the biography of a man who spent several years in a POW camp in North Vietnam. He was an avid golfer, and every afternoon he played a full eighteen holes in his mind. Using a stick, he walked around his tiny cell, swinging his arms as best he could. He saw himself getting in the golf cart and chugging to the next hole. He visualized every swing of every hole. When he finally returned home, he took up his game as if he'd never been interrupted.

All this demonstrates the power of meditation, the potential of visualization, and the truth of the proverbial adage, "As [a man] thinketh in his heart, so is he" (Prov. 23:7 KJV).

Who created our brains with their incredible complexity? Who gave us the ability of painting frescos on the walls of our mind? Who made the imagination?

I'm not really an advocate of the philosophy that sloganizes, "If you can conceive it and believe it, you'll receive it." It's not that automatic or naive. But the Lord certainly wants us to contemplate His Word in our minds, using all the mental powers He gave us. Our minds are an amazing bit of God's creative genius. They process thought, but they also visualize and imagine. The daydreams and fantasies of our fallen natures are often harmful; but there's tremendous power in the sanctified use of imagination and visualization.

Scripture memory allows us to practice spiritual contemplation. Jesus said in Matthew 22:37, we must love the Lord our God with all our hearts, souls, and *minds*.

- "Be renewed in the spirit of your *mind*" (Eph. 4:23 NKJV, emphasis mine here and in the following verses).
- "You will keep him in perfect peace, whose *mind* is stayed on You, because he trusts in You" (Isa. 26:3 NKJV).
- "Let this *mind* be in you which was also in Christ Jesus" (Phil. 2:5 NKJV).
- "Set your *mind* on things above, not on things on the earth" (Col. 3:2 NKJV).
- "For those who live according to the flesh set their *minds* on the things of the flesh, but those who live according to the Spirit, the things of the Spirit. For to be carnally *minded* is death, but to be spiritually *minded* is life and peace" (Rom. 8:5–6 NKJV).
- "God has not given us a spirit of fear, but of power and of love and of a sound *mind*" (2 Tim. 1:7 NKJV).
- "Therefore gird up the loins of your *mind,* be sober, and rest your hope fully upon the grace that is to be brought to you at the revelation of Jesus Christ" (1 Pet. 1:13 NKJV).

- And Romans 12:2 tells us to be transformed by the renewing of our *minds*.

The simplest way of implementing these precepts is by printing God's Word on the billboards of our psyches. Think of the mysterious hand that scribbled the terrifying message of doom and destruction across the walls of Belshazzar's palace in Daniel 5. The same hand can write a positive, hope-filled message of life on the walls of our intellects whenever we learn the Scriptures by heart.

The apostle Paul told us in Colossians 3:16 to let the Word of God dwell in us richly; and in the Old Testament the Lord promised, "This is the covenant that I will make with the house of Israel after those days, says the LORD: I will put My law in their minds, and write it on their hearts; and I will be their God, and they shall be My people" (Jer. 31:33 NKJV).

Listen to this translation of Deuteronomy 6:4–7: "Listen, Israel! The LORD our God is the only true God! So love the LORD your God with all your heart, soul, and strength. Memorize his laws and tell them to your children over and over again" (CEV).

Deuteronomy 11:18 says, "Memorize these laws and think about them" (CEV). And Psalm 119:11 says, "Your word I have hidden in my heart, that I might not sin against You" (NKJV).

Scripture memory enables us to maintain our mental equilibrium and spiritual vitality. We can see the Scripture in our minds, picturing its scenes, hearing its words as if spoken just to us, rolling them over in our minds like rocks in a tumbler. We're transported to green pastures, still waters, Galilean storms, Judeans hills, Roman jails, golden streets, and to the very throne of God Himself.

When you memorize biblical texts, you're putting frames around the verses and hanging them on the walls of your inner library. And you'll find as you visualize them that you're always in the picture.

One night I was worried about someone I loved. At length I knew I had to get some sleep, for staying up all night wouldn't help the situation; it'd only leave me exhausted the next day when I needed fresh energy to deal with it. I couldn't relax in bed, but I thought I might be able to rest on the sofa if only I could corral my runaway thoughts. But my mind wouldn't cooperate, imagining the worst and visualizing every terrible scenario. Finally I decided to manhandle my thoughts and force them in a different direction. Tossing on the sofa, I began to repeat the Twenty-third Psalm, which I had memorized many years before:

> The LORD is my shepherd; I shall not want. He maketh me to lie down in green pastures: he leadeth me beside the still waters. He restoreth my soul: he leadeth me in the paths of righteousness for his name's sake. Yea, though I walk through the valley of the shadow of death, I will fear no evil: for thou art with me. (KJV)

When I got to the end, I started again from the beginning. My mind began to visualize those green pastures, to see and sense the Good Shepherd, to know His presence in the dark valley, to claim His promises of goodness and mercy.

As my mind relaxed, so did my body; and I was able to sleep.

Later I thought to myself, *What if I had never known Psalm 23?* What if someone had not led me to memorize Psalm 23 when I was in the second grade? What would I have done? Where would I have turned?

Many people have told me of experiencing the same peace while contemplating Psalm 23 word by word; and just today I read in the newspaper about a man who, during a time of deepest trouble, quoted the Twenty-third Psalm to himself 100 times in a single day.

Dr. Martin Seligman of the University of Pennsylvania is perhaps the world's foremost expert on optimism and motivation. In his groundbreaking book, *Learned Optimism,* he suggests that depression is primarily the result of wrong thinking. He writes, "Depression . . . is caused by conscious negative thoughts. There is no deep underlying disorder to be rooted out: not unresolved childhood conflicts, not our unconscious anger, and not even our brain chemistry. Emotion comes directly from what we think: Think 'I am in danger' and you feel anxiety. Think 'I am being trespassed against' and you feel anger. Think 'Loss' and you feel sadness. . . . If we change these habits of thought, we will cure depression."[5]

Scripture memory is our most powerful tool in changing our habits of thought, and the internalized truths of God's Word keep us mentally healthy. It's the greatest secret I know to personal resiliency. It molds our thoughts, and our thoughts shape our lives; for as we think in our hearts, so we are.

If our "little gray cells" are such an important thing about us, and if the Holy Scriptures are the very thoughts of God Himself, then Bible verses represent the most healing, clarifying, bolstering, uplifting data we can insert into our brains. The power of Scripture is unlike anything else on earth. It's a force to be reckoned with, containing intrinsic power, high enough to give us insight, deep enough to give us peace, wide enough to mold our personalities, and strong enough to bear us through horrendous days.

Someone once told me that Scripture memory accelerates the transformation process in our lives. It's like a special additive that exponentially increases the efficiency of sanctification. By internalizing Bible verses, we're mainstreaming God's thoughts into our conscious, subconscious, and unconscious logic.

I don't know about you, but that's what I constantly need.

Your instructions are written on my heart.

(Psalm 40:8 NLT)

FIVE

GETTING SCRIPTURE INTO PRACTICE

One night several years ago I sat up into the wee hours, engrossed in a book I'd picked up at a yard sale. *In the Presence of Mine Enemies* was the memoir of Vietnam POW Howard Rutledge, who was shot down over North Vietnam on November 28, 1965. When his plane was hit, Howard bailed out, but he descended into thick mud near a large village and was soon surrounded by a crowd welding knives, machetes, and sticks. Forming a ring around him, the townspeople blocked his escape and descended on him, pounding him with blows, stripping off his clothing, and dragging him into their little jail, half dead. Shortly thereafter, he was transported to the infamous Hanoi Hilton where he was brutally interrogated and tortured.

Howard described how, in an initial set of tortures, his legs were forced into rough shackles, with his arms hog-tied in an excruciating position. He was deprived of clothing, food, and sleep and forced to lie on a cold slab in a mucky cell. The walls, floors, and ceilings were caked with filth, and a large rat shared his space.

Until his incarceration Howard had felt little concern for spiritual things; but now he desperately tried to recall snatches of Bible verses, hymns, or sermons he had heard in his childhood. Fortunately as a youngster he had attended a church in Tulsa, Oklahoma, with a Sunday school that had stressed the importance of Scripture memory. There in the POW camp, he racked his brain for every single verse he could recall. During the rare moments when he could communicate with other POWs, he found them seeking to do the same.

"Everyone knew the Lord's Prayer and the Twenty-third Psalm," he said, "but the camp favorite verse that everyone recalled first and quoted most often is found in the Book of John, third chapter, sixteenth verse: For God so loved the world, that He gave His only begotten Son, that whosoever believeth in Him should not perish, but have everlasting life."

With a friend's help, Howard even managed to reconstruct verses 17 and 18.

Howard wrote, "How I struggled to recall those Scriptures and hymns! I had spent my first eighteen years in a Southern Baptist Sunday School, and I was amazed at how much I could recall; regrettably, I had not seen the importance of memorizing verses from the Bible. . . . Now, when I needed them, it was too late. I never dreamed that I would spend almost seven years (five of them in solitary confinement) in a prison in North Vietnam or that thinking about one memorized verse could have made a whole day bearable. One portion of a verse I did remember was, 'Thy word have I hid in my heart.' How often I wished I had really worked to hide God's Word in my heart. I put my mind to work."

In his memoirs Howard described days and nights of tortures that made my skin crawl as I read about them; but he also testified of being able, as time progressed, to recall more and more Bible verses from the recesses of his mind. His recollection wasn't word perfect, but he was amazed at how many phrases and sentences from the Bible lay buried deep in his memory, waiting to be discovered.

Those Bible verses literally kept Howard Rutledge from losing his mind. The memorized snippets of Scripture in his brain were potent. They faced down death, rallied his spirits, steeled his nerves, and tapped into the deepest strength known in the universe. They beat back the torture, stifled the despair, subdued the terrors he felt, and maintained his sanity even when he was immobilized for days in a stifling hut, chained to a metal frame, lying in his own waste, and covered with ants, flies, and biting insects.

Those verses, long ago learned by heart, proved more restorative than any tonic. They dispensed strength and were sufficient to the pain; and they bolstered his mind and his mood with the strongest thoughts of an omniscient God in the midst of humanity's most sadistic ravings. They were the reason he came home alive.

"That first New Year's Eve in Heartbreak Hotel," he wrote, "I had resolved never to be without a Bible again. Those verses of God's Word that I had memorized or that I had scrounged from other prisoners' memories had been a living source of strength in my life."[6]

Most of us will never be POWs in a concentration camp, but all of us occasionally check into Heartbreak Hotel. Life is hard, full of anguishing moments and dangerous temptations. We need strong minds—brains that think clearly, emotions that remain calm and steady.

Bible verses, committed to memory and applied by the Holy Spirit, are the most powerful medications in the whole world. They're a balm for sore hearts, an elixir for low spirits, an immunization for bad habits, a booster shot of high spirits, a pick-me-up for dreary days, and a stimulant for positive nerves.

How many Bible verses could you reconstruct from your memory banks if push came to shove? How about your children? Are they hiding away God's Word in their hearts, storing up the precious seeds of the Scriptures against the coming famine? Do your teenagers know the Bible verses they need to withstand the temptations they'll face?

The Bible was written to be memorized. Take Psalm 25, for example. If you'll turn there in your Bible and notice it, it has twenty-two verses. The Hebrew alphabet has twenty-two letters; so when we find a passage like this with twenty-two verses, it's likely an acrostic. In the original Hebrew of Psalm 25, for example, verse 1 begins with the Hebrew equivalent of our letter *A*. Verse 2, with the Hebrew equivalent of our letter *B*. And so forth.

Why is that important? It was a mnemonic, a device to aid in memorization. This psalm was intended for memorization. Its message was so important that the writer wanted to make it easy to memorize.

The longest chapter in the Bible—Psalm 119—is actually composed of twenty-two segments arranged as an extended acrostic. The passage about the wise woman in Proverbs 31 likewise has twenty-two segments.

In other words, these were composed to be memorized. In the days before the printing press, many people didn't have access to their own copies of the Bible so they memorized vast portions of God's Word. How tragic that now, with all our modern versions and translations, we're memorizing it less and less, if at all.

But remember, whenever we store away a verse in our minds, it becomes a concealed weapon. It's a light, a lamp, a vault of gold, a hive of honey, and a two-edged sword. It's available day and night for practical purposes. It helps us "fix" our thoughts, and we fix our thoughts by fixing them on Jesus via His praiseworthy Word.

Fix your thoughts on Jesus.

(Hebrews 3:1 NIV)

SIX

THE STARTING POINT: FIXING OUR THOUGHTS

Hans Hugenberg considered himself the most creative horticultur-
alist and landscaper in Italy. His formal gardens graced some of
the country's most exclusive estates; and for two decades he served as the
chief private consultant for the Italian government, dispensing expensive
advice on everything from the design of national parks to the layout of
official residences.

Hans had a prize-winning style that was unique in Europe. His
gardens extended in balanced and regular patterns yet with a twist and
flair that was distinctively his own. He blended sunlight with shade
and shadows, sunken ponds with sloping fields and tunneling arbors,
straight lines with curving pathways and curious steps.

He was a master with only one regret. He had no garden of his own.
He tended the gardens of the nation, but he himself lived in an apartment without acreage, for he traveled too widely, gambled too frequently,

drank too much, and stayed too busy for anything more than a six-room flat in Milan.

Then at age forty-nine, he retired from professional life to become a homeowner and a man of leisure. He purchased a little villa forty-three kilometers from Rome. It was a small palazzo near a country byroad with a quaintly designed garden in the rear. But the garden was overgrown, crawling with rodents, and infested with weeds. It had been neglected and needed the touch of a master's hand.

Hans knew what to do. The garden needed a focal point, a centerpiece. He traveled to Naples, Florence, and Turin, visiting the handful of sculptors whom he most admired. Finally, in Venice in the shop of his old pal Francesco, he found what he'd been looking for. It was a ten-foot statute of Jesus Christ at the moment of the ascension. Christ's hands were lifted upward in blessing, His feet on tiptoe as though leaving the world, but His eyes gazed downward as though looking lovingly at the disciples He was leaving behind.

Hans transported the statuary to his garden, where he cleared away the debris, laid a foundation, and set it in the very center. He began designing the garden around the statue. Every plant, every path, every pond was arranged in correspondence and symmetry with the statue of Christ. Every tree and flower was selected to maintain the particular proportion and uniformity created by the statue of the ascending Christ. Every line and lawn led the eye to the uplifted hands and the downgazing eyes of Christ. The weeds were pulled, and the rats were evicted— all under the gaze of the centrality of Christ.

Jesus Christ was the centerpiece around which the garden was cultivated.[7]

That's the key to our mental gardens as well. Left to themselves, our mentality becomes overgrown with weeds and infested with rodents. Without Christ our thoughts tend toward evil, filled with impure imaginations and harmful attitudes and misguided motives. But when we turn over ownership of our lives to Christ, He begins to transform our minds and to cultivate holiness and happiness. Our minds become His garden, centered on Him and sown with the bulbs of the Bible and the seeds of Scripture.

After all, the human brain is arguably the climax of God's creation, the most incredible invention in His universe. It's a fabulous, living super-computer with unfathomable circuitry and unimaginable complexity, a collection of billions of neurons, each as complex as a small computer—like having one hundred billion computers inside your cranium. And they're all interconnected. One scientist said that the number of connec-tions within one human brain rivals the number of stars and galaxies in the entire universe.

Sometimes I wonder if some of those connections don't occasion-ally short-circuit in my case. I feel befuddled, make wrong decisions, forget important engagements, give foolish advice, and let in impure or discouraging influences. Our thoughts get us into more trouble than a sack full of demons. Whenever we say the wrong thing, yield to tempta-tions, or react with foolish choices, the point of origin is the brain. The mind itself is the battleground of the soul, and our thinking often gets out of whack.

There are a couple of ways to fix our thoughts when they're in bad repair.

Hebrews 3:1 says we should "fix [our] thoughts on Jesus, the apostle and high priest whom we confess" (NIV); and Philippians 4:8 says, "Fix your thoughts on what is true, and honorable, and right, and pure, and lovely, and admirable. Think about things that are excellent and worthy of praise" (NLT).

Scripture memory and meditation is the key to a healthy mind for those who have given their lives to Jesus Christ and centered their thoughts on Him. The Holy Bible isn't just a great book; it's in a class by itself: a book authored by the Creator God, through the agency of human beings, who were guided by the Holy Spirit in their writings.

The Bible's double authorship is utterly unique in the history of literature. The whole supposition of Christianity is that there is a God, that He made us, that He loves us, that He is concerned about our lives, and that He is capable of communicating with us. He has done so using a method so extraordinary, yet so simple, that only God Himself could have conceived it. He chose forty or so human beings who lived during a span of fifteen hundred or so years, and He superintended the sentences they wrote, down to the very words and syllables—yet without suspending their own intellects, personalities, or circumstances.

We can therefore say that every word in the Bible is of human authorship, yet it is all divinely given. Its heavenly authorship gives it a transcendent, timeless authority; and its human origin touches our lives in a timely, tangible way.

Bible verses are high-powered doses of truth that mainline God's wisdom into our reasoning. They convert the soul, teach the simple, rejoice the heart, and enlighten the eyes (Ps. 19:7–9). They teach, reprove, correct, and instruct, making us profitable in every good work (2 Tim. 3:16–17). They fill our minds with the kind of realities that produce prosperity and success in every good work (Josh. 1:8; Ps. 1:1–3). Bible verses are our counselors and our delights, ready to revive us when we're fainting, guide us when we're confused, and strengthen us when we're weak (Ps. 119:24–28).

They are our comfort in affliction (Ps. 119:50), our songs for the journey (Ps. 119:54), and our most valuable asset (Ps. 119:72); for when we read and study God's Word, we're cultivating a relationship with Him who made us, who loved us, who gave Himself for us on Calvary, and who rose again that we might inherit eternal life. As we study His Word, we're listening to Him, conversing with Him face-to-face, as it were, as a man speaks to his friend.

Psalm 37:3 (NKJV) tell us to "feed on His faithfulness," and as we inscribe God's Word on the tablets of our minds, we're able to do that in the sweet pastures of His truth. The Bible becomes portable, and we can take it wherever we take our minds, our brains, and our thoughts.

Christian worker Bob Foster calls Scripture memory "the daily habit of supplying the subconscious with God's material to chew upon."[8] Specific Bible verses are seeds that produce a crop. They germinate quickly and almost instantly began improving the quality of the soul. By memorizing the 100 verses suggested in this book, you'll immediately experience seven remarkable benefits that will change your life. Memorizing Scripture gives us:

1. Clearer thoughts.
2. Steadier nerves.
3. Healthier emotions.
4. Purer habits.
5. Happier homes.
6. Greater respect.
7. Eternal optimism.

Isn't that worth at least five minutes a day?

A good person produces good things from the treasury of a good heart.

(Matthew 12:35 NLT)

SEVEN

SEVEN IMMEDIATE BENEFITS OF SCRIPTURE MEMORY, PART 1

A woman caught in the Pacific conflicts of World War II was imprisoned by the Japanese in China and placed in a concentration camp where copies of the Bible were forbidden, punishable by pain of death. Somehow, however, she acquired a small copy of the Gospel of John, and every night she pulled her head beneath the covers and, using a small flashlight, began memorizing the book. As she memorized a page, she would tear it out, take it with her to the waterspout, dissolve it with soap, and flush it down the drain. In this way she later said, "John and I parted company."

Just before the prisoners were released, a reporter for *Time* Magazine entered the camp to interview some of the detainees. Later this reporter was standing at the gates as the prisoners came out. Most of them shuffled along, eyes downcast, looking like zombies. This little lady, however, was beaming and bright as a button.

"I wonder if they managed to brainwash her?" someone asked.

"No," said the reporter. "God washed her brain."[9]

The reporter was simply observing what Jesus had said just before He was seized by the Roman soldiers who crucified Him. In His great, final high-priestly prayer in John 17, He prayed for His disciples, saying, "Sanctify them by Your truth. Your Word is truth" (v. 17 NKJV). The word *sanctify* means "make them Your holy, happy people, a people consecrated wholly to You, Your representatives in this world." It's the Word—the Truth—that accomplishes this as we hear it, learn it, believe it, and heed it.

Scripture memory gives us clearer thoughts. Internalized Scripture keeps our minds in good working order. John Ruskin, the brilliant British social critic whose views about art and architecture were influential during the Victorian and Edwardian periods of English history, testifies to this. Ruskin was an author, poet, and creative thinker; and today Ruskin College in Oxford is named for him. Leo Tolstoy described him as "one of those rare men who think with their heart."

When he was young, Ruskin's mother insisted that he memorize seventeen different chapters of the Bible, word perfect, six of them from the Old Testament. She also assigned an additional eight psalms.

When he was fifty-five, Ruskin said that memorizing these chapters had "established my soul in life." He said that though afterward he learned many things from many teachers, the "installation" of the Bible into his brain became "the most precious and on the whole the one essential part of all my education. For the chapters became indeed strictly conclusive and productive to me in all modes of thought."[10]

All truth is God's truth, but Scripture is His *revealed* truth and provides the intellectual foundation for all the rest. It provides the historical, philosophical, theological, and psychological scaffolding within which all other facts become cohesive. It reveals the wisdom of God regarding everything from daily life to eternal life. Without the engraving of

Scripture in our minds, we're left with a brain filled with the rantings and ravings of a confused intellect.

At the beginning of His ministry, when Jesus faced satanic temptation in the wilderness, He quoted verses He'd learned from the Old Testament. Throughout His ministry Jesus recited extensively from the Hebrew Scriptures. And in the last, stress-filled, anguished, painful moments of His life, Jesus again quoted Old Testament Scriptures He'd previously memorized, such as: "Into Your hands I commit My spirit" (Luke 23:46 NKJV) and "My God, my God, why hast thou forsaken me?" (Matt. 27:46 KJV). These are direct quotes from Psalm 31 and Psalm 22. Our Lord was quoting memorized Scripture on the cross, taking the Old Testament prayers of the psalmist David and making them His own.

If memorized Bible verses enabled Jesus to think clearly during six torturous hours on the cross, think of how they can help us through the stress and strain of each day. When we recall Scriptures, they become like sanitizers of the brain, washing our minds in a bath of praise.

Scripture memory gives us steadier nerves. Specific Bible verses stored away in our minds serve as the shock absorbers of life, giving us steadier nerves and calmer spirits.

As I'm preparing this chapter, I'm grappling with a deep disappointment in my own life, one I had not expected to face. It's threatened to preoccupy my thoughts, rob my joy, and disrupt my peace. But the Lord has given me a verse to memorize, and I have it posted on the dashboard of my car. Since I'm in and out of my car several times a day, I'm reviewing it constantly; and I've even created a little song that helps me remember it. This verse, now so precious to me, is Ephesians 1:11: "In him we were also chosen, having been predestined according to the plan of him who works out everything in conformity with the purpose of his will" (NIV). It seems to me that this verse is a duplication of Romans 8:28 NKJV ("We know that all things work together for good to those who love God"), only from an "above" perspective.

Romans 8:28 is from a below perspective, telling us that here on earth all things work for our good. Ephesians 1:11 is from God's perspective, telling us that all things work together in conformity with the purpose of His will in order that we might be for the praise of His glory (v. 12).

I don't think I'll ever forget this week with its unexpected heartache and my wonderful discovery of Ephesians 1:11, which I'm committing to memory.

Some time ago I read the story of Dwayne and Bonnie Wheat, whose lives changed forever on February 22, 1991, when a police officer awoke them in the early hours with the tragic news that their daughter, Charla, had been murdered. Bonnie later testified that it was the power of memorized Scripture that kept her from going insane during the days that followed. "In those days I could not read the Bible and focus on it long enough for it to make sense," she said, "but it was God's Word that was already in my heart that ministered to me. I am so thankful for that. It was things like, 'Be still and know that I am God,' and 'Thou wilt keep him in perfect peace whose mind is stayed on Thee. . . .' God used those Scriptures to show me that we just had to be still and let God be God."[11]

If you want steadier nerves, learn the power of inscribing on your heart those Bible verses God gives you in moments of need. "The Scriptures were written to teach and encourage us by giving us hope. God is the one who makes us patient and cheerful" (Rom. 15:4–5 CEV).

Every student well-trained in God's kingdom is like
the owner of a general store who can put his hands
on anything you need, old or new, exactly when you need it.

(Matthew 13:52 *The Message*)

SEVEN IMMEDIATE BENEFITS OF SCRIPTURE MEMORY, PART 2

B ut there's more.

Scripture memory also gives us healthier emotions. I'm convinced that little biblical capsules (memory verses) are the best medicine for sustained emotional health. Like most people, I've struggled with my temper in times past, but no anger management technique is as powerful as memorizing verses like Proverbs 29:11: "A fool gives full vent to his anger, but a wise man keeps himself under control" (NIV).

If you struggle with depression, you'll find a potent antidote in memorizing Psalm 42, or the opening verses of Psalm 103. If you're anxious, internalize Philippians 4:6–7. If you struggle with a low self-image, get Romans 12:1–8 into your noggin. If you're hard to get along with, irritable, and unpersonable, memorize Romans 12:17–21. If you lack discipline and self-control, a bunch of verses in Proverbs are just waiting to be planted in your head. If you struggle with guilt, read 1 John 1:7–9 and quote it to yourself until it penetrates your thinking and changes the core of your heart.

The sturdy truths of God's Word will enable you to keep your wits even in crises. Several years ago in Sweden, I found an English-speaking book telling one of the most gripping stories I've ever read: *Evidence Not Seen: One Woman's Faith in a Japanese POW Camp.* The author, Darlene Deibler Rose, was captured in Asia, like the woman I mentioned earlier, by the Japanese during World War II; and her experiences were also truly harrowing. She went into the camp with her Bible, but the guards took it away; however, they could not remove the memorized Scriptures from her mind.

"Much time was passed repeating Scripture," Darlene wrote. "As a child and young person, I had had a driving compulsion to memorize the written Word. In the cell I was grateful now for those days in Vacation Bible School, when I had memorized many single verses, complete chapters, and Psalms, as well as whole books of the Bible. In the years that followed, I reviewed the Scriptures often. The Lord fed me with the Living Bread that had been stored against the day when fresh supply was cut off by the loss of my Bible. He brought daily comfort and encouragement—yes, and joy—to my heart through the knowledge of the Word."

Darlene continued, "Paul, the apostle, wrote that it was through the comfort of the Scriptures that he had hope and steadfastness of heart to believe God. I had never needed the Scriptures more than in these months on death row, but since so much of His Word was there in my heart, it was not the punishment the Kempeitai had anticipated when they took my Bible."[12]

In the book *Who's in Charge?* pastor Ben Patterson claims that memorizing selected Scriptures has helped him stay mentally healthy amid the rigors of criticism in the ministry. He said, "When I was young, I never won any awards for Sunday school Scripture memory contests. Someone else always rode away on the ten-speed bicycle at the end of the year. But in the last three years I've discovered that Scripture can give voice to things I don't know how to express. It transforms the things churning inside me and brings real healing to my soul.

"One summer I memorized the twelfth chapter of Hebrews. At the time the entire chapter seemed autobiographical: running the race set before us, remembering Jesus, who endured the cross, who didn't lose heart though scorned by men. The chapter reminded me that pain is a discipline God uses in my life: I was in training, and the pain caused by criticism was my coach."[13]

Bible verses, well memorized, are stabilizers for our nerves, strengthening our attitudes and improving our emotions.

Scripture memory also gives us purer habits. The practice of memorizing and meditating on the Bible is the primary way to accelerate spiritual growth in your life. It speeds up the transformation process and leads to holier habits. After all, spiritual maturity is simply thinking more as God thinks; so as we implant His thoughts into our minds, using Scripture memory, and as we use the process of meditation to convert those verses into regular thought patterns, we're developing the mind of Christ (Phil. 2:5), yielding mature thoughts, pure habits, and holier lives. The psalmist said, "Your word I have hidden in my heart, that I might not sin against You" (Ps. 119:11 NKJV).

When John Crawford was in the navy, one of the games played aboard ship was the anchor pool. Each participating sailor would put in his money and guess what time they would drop anchor. The exact time was recorded in the ship's log, and the one with the closest guess got the money. It seemed like an innocent game, and the other sailors encouraged him to join in. It was tempting, and he wanted to be a good sport. But he knew they also wanted his money and that gambling wasn't a habit he wanted to begin.

As the temptation intensified, John decided to steel himself with memorized Scriptures. He chose Proverbs 13:11: "Wealth gotten by vanity shall be diminished; but he that gathereth by labour shall increase" (KJV), and Proverbs 23:5: "Wilt thou set thine eyes upon that which is not? For riches certainly make themselves wings; they fly away, as an eagle toward heaven" (KJV).

Not only did those verses fortify John against the temptations of the moment, they enabled him to establish lifelong patterns regarding integrity, honesty, and the role of money in his life.[14]

I think of memorized Scripture as divine detergent in the brain, constantly washing my mind and cleansing and clarifying my thoughts.

The psalmist said, "I've banked your promises in the vault of my heart so I won't sin myself bankrupt" (Ps. 119:11 *The Message*). No temptation catches us devoid of potential Bible verses specifically designed to combat it. God has given us texts to cover any temptation and all sin. If we struggle with depression, we have Psalm 42. If we struggle with materialism and greed, we have 1 Timothy 6. If our besetting sin is a foul mouth or an angry spirit, we have Ephesians 4. If it's lust, pornography, or immorality, learn the first part of Ephesians 5.

The Bible is an offensive weapon, the sword of the Spirit. By quoting Old Testament texts He'd memorized, Jesus struck down every temptation Satan flung at Him on Temptation Mount. And we can do the same. Determine your weakest links, then search out verses to combat those struggles. Memorize them diligently; and you'll find, in the words of an old evangelist, that sin will keep you from the Bible, or the Bible will keep you from sin.

"The instruction of his God is in his heart," says Psalm 37:31, "his steps do not falter."

Write them on the tablet of your heart.

(Proverbs 3:3)

NINE

SEVEN IMMEDIATE BENEFITS OF SCRIPTURE MEMORY, PART 3

The government of Norway recently announced construction of an enormous doomsday vault in the Arctic, a sort of "Noah's ark" for seeds in the event a global catastrophe wiped out the earth's vegetation. The cornerstone for the Svalbard Global Seed Vault was laid near the town of Longyearbyen, 620 miles from the North Pole, with the prime ministers of Norway, Sweden, Denmark, Finland, and Iceland in attendance. The vault is designed to stockpile as many as three million of the world's crop seeds, which will be packaged in foil and stored at cold temperatures. Researchers claim the seeds could last hundreds, even thousands, of years.

Our minds are vaults especially designed to stockpile the seeds of God's Word. We never know when we'll be hit by a catastrophic loss, faced with a staggering problem, or challenged by a formidable foe. We don't know what our children will encounter during their life's journey, but we do know that the simple seeds of Scripture are priceless assets in times of drought, doubt, and difficulty. We can leave our children no inheritance more valuable than the legacy of God's Word. It gives us clearer thoughts, steadier nerves, healthier emotions, purer habits, and better environments.

And that's the fifth benefit of Scripture memory. It gives us happier homes. One of the by-products of internalizing God's Word is a brighter home life, for as you mull over the transformational truths of God, you become a more functional and wiser person; and as your children do the same, they learn the secrets of healthier relationships.

One of the most mysterious and commanding figures in Christian history is the virgin Mary, mother of Jesus. We're full of curiosity about her, for the Bible gives us only fleeting data about her life's story. But if you read carefully, you'll notice she must have been a great Scripture memorizer. In Luke 1, when the angel Gabriel told her she would bear the Messiah, she hurried to the home of her relative, Elizabeth, and there she broke out in one of the Bible's greatest prayers of praise—the Magnificat in Luke 1:46–55. It drew heavily on Old Testament Bible verses, and we get the impression that Mary was a student of Old Testament Scriptures, with a rich treasury of verses packed away in her experience. She knew how to ponder these things in her heart.

When she burst into a prayer of praise, it was composed largely of verses she had stored away through the years. We can also assume she frequently quoted those verses to her firstborn as He was growing up. It's incredible to think that Mary's commitment to Scripture memory was perhaps one of the reasons God selected her to raise the Messiah. The precious verses of God's Word filled her heart and undoubtedly filled her home.

Deuteronomy 6 tells us to talk about the Scriptures when we lie down and when we rise up, when we sit at home and when we walk along the way. This assumes that we have ready mental reference to the Scriptures so that we'll be able to recall the right verse for the right occasion.

One of the first verses my wife and I tried to teach our children was Proverbs 20:11: "Even a child is known by his deeds, whether what he does is pure and right" (NKJV).

I suggest teaching your child memory verses by hook or by crook. If your church, school, or Bible club has a Scripture memory program, jump in with both feet. If not, develop your own, using the verses in this book. As I said in chapter 2, I learned many of the verses I treasure today in an incentive-based school program; so don't be afraid to use incentives. I know one woman who memorized the entire Sermon on the Mount because her teacher offered her five dollars (back in the days when five dollars was a lot of money). She later said that she wouldn't give a thousand times that amount now for the joy of having learned those three chapters, Matthew 5, 6, and 7.

Sixth, Scripture memory enhances our reputations. It augments the respect with which people view us. Isaiah 50:4 says, "The Lord GOD has given Me the tongue of the learned, that I should know how to speak a word in season to him who is weary" (NKJV).

Job's friends told him, "Your words have upheld him who was stumbling, and you have strengthened the feeble knees" (Job 4:4 NKJV).

Publisher Brad Waggoner grew up on a ranch where all the farmhands and cowboys carried cans of tobacco in their back pockets. Later in college he met a group of Christians—Navigators—who also had something outlined in their hip pockets. But it wasn't tobacco. These men carried around packets containing memory verses, which they worked on learning at every spare moment. Enticed to try it for himself, Brad started by memorizing three verses. "I couldn't believe what an effect they had on me, on both my thinking and my talking. It seasoned my conversation with salt."

Brad was so motivated by the experience that he's become a lifelong advocate of Scripture memory, and the verses he's learned over the years are reflected every day in the conversations he has with friends and coworkers.

Where do we get the wisdom to speak a word in season to those who are weary? How can we know what to say when someone is stumbling or in need of inner strength? Our ability to wisely dispense needed words is directly proportional to our knowledge of *His* words and of His *Word*.

In my book of hymn stories, *Then Sings My Soul,* I tell the remarkable story of Fanny Crosby, who was born in 1820 about sixty miles north of New York City. Her father died shortly after her birth, and she herself was blinded in infancy by a careless doctor treating her eyes. But as a result of her blindness, Fanny developed a phenomenal memory. She memorized vast segments of the Scripture—whole books of the Bible including all four Gospels. She later said that whenever she wanted to read a portion of Scripture, she turned a little button in her mind, and the appropriate passage would flow through her brain like a recorded tape.

After she came to the Lord, that vast reservoir of memorized Scripture became the nurturing fountain for her hymns. She would compose hymn after hymn in her brain and retain them with perfect memory, then go to her publishers and dictate them one after another. During her ninety-four years of life, she wrote approximately nine thousand hymns, more than anyone else in known church history.

Whenever she wrote a hymn, she prayed that God would use it to bring men and women to Christ. She had a goal of winning a million people to Christ through the agency of her hymns, and she kept careful track of every story she heard of someone being saved through her hymns. To this day someone somewhere on earth is singing, playing, or listening to her hymns practically every moment day and night—hymns such as "Blessed Assurance," "All the Way My Savior Leads Me," "To God Be the Glory," and "Near the Cross."

When your mind is a virtual repository of Scripture, you'll seldom be at a loss for something to say, and you'll seldom say the wrong thing; for you will have the wisdom from above at your disposal on every occasion.

Finally, Scripture memory makes us eternal optimists. It gives ultimate hope and modulates us into eternal optimists. There's a promise in the Bible for every contingency in life; and our faith grows as we find those specific promises that meet our specific needs, commit them to memory, mull over them, claim them by faith, and absorb them into our spiritual bloodstream. Even death itself is no match for God's precious promises of resurrection, eternal life, and everlasting joy.

When I was a college student, I had the privilege of being taught by Ruth Bell Graham, who opened her home to me on several occasions; and I was impressed by her personal "collection" of memorized verses. "Some people collect paintings and some collect coins," she said, in effect, "but I collect Bible verses."

For many years Billy and Ruth Graham worked alongside Cliff and Billie Barrows. When Cliff's wife, Billie, was diagnosed with advanced cancer, Billy and Ruth Graham came for a visit, along with Mr. and Mrs. George Beverly Shea. Sitting by the fire, these old friends spent the afternoon reminiscing and speaking of God's faithfulness. They had traveled around the world together many times over the years, preaching the gospel of Christ. The tenderness and laughter of their recollections was tinged with the sadness that one of them, Billie, would soon be departing for heaven.

Late in the day the conversation died down; and in the quietness Ruth began quoting Romans 8: What then shall we say to these things? If God is for us, who can be against us? He who did not spare His own Son, but delivered Him up for us all, how shall He not with Him also freely give us all things? . . . Who shall separate us from the love of Christ? (31–32, 35 NKJV). And she went on to quote the rest of the passage by heart.

"These words were almost stunning to me," the Barrows' daughter, BettyRuth Seera later told me. "It was a very familiar passage . . . but never before had I realized the depth of comfort and hope they offered. I determined that day to memorize this passage and to follow Aunt Ruth's example to be ready to give an account for the hope that is within me."[15]

Only as we engrave the Bible's rich passages on the walls of our hearts can we be ready, in season and out of season, to share a word timely spoken.

When I was in college in the 1970s, Bill Gothard was conducting popular week-long seminars across the country, and a bunch of us students took our spring break to go to Philadelphia and attend his conference. I still have the notes, and many of Gothard's insights had a big impact on me. The thing I remember most clearly was his definition of wisdom. Wisdom, Gothard said, was seeing life from God's point of view. And then he went on to emphasize the importance of Scripture memory and meditation. Gothard said that meditation is the practice of memorizing, visualizing, and personalizing Scripture.

As we faithfully memorize and meditate on Scripture, the Holy Spirit will gradually remold our minds until we see things and evaluate life increasingly from God's point of view, and that's the essence of wisdom.

Keep my teaching with you all the time; write it on your heart.

(Proverbs 7:3 GNT)

TEN

YOU CAN DO IT!

Not long ago I spoke at a luncheon in Asheville, North Carolina. The setting was the clubhouse of a golf course, and the views across the mountains were fabulous. Many of those in attendance had moved to the North Carolina high country for their retirement years, and I was seated beside a gracious woman in her eighties. As we chatted, I brought up the subject of Scripture memory.

"Oh," she said, "I found it so easy to memorize when I was younger, but now it is hard to get my brain to retain the words."

I agreed, but I suggested we can still work on it. "God has made our brains so they mature and develop over time," I said. "When we're young, we have good memorizers because there is so much material to learn. When we're older, our memorizers slow down, but our wisdomizers speed up because we have to sort out all the information we've previously acquired. We have to use it correctly. But we can still memorize Bible verses even if it takes longer to do so."

"I'm so glad you told me that," she said.

The 100 verses in this book are for people from one to one hundred. My four-year-old grandson, Elijah, is learning memory verses, and he can beat me four to one. But as long as our minds are in reasonable working order, we can memorize. I can prove it to you. Do you know your phone number? If you moved to a new house, don't you think you could learn your address? If you welcomed a grandchild into the world, don't you think you'd learn and remember his or her name? I have ten grandchildren. Sometimes when I'm calling one of them, I go through a handful of names (including the dog's). But I really do know the name of each child and eventually come up with the right one.

Can you learn the security code on your home protection system? How about your post office box? Today's date? The name of the new store that opened down the road? The name of the neighbor who moved in across the street? The day and time of the new television program you've become interested in, and the names of the chief characters? The score of last week's football game? The BCS rankings? Your Internet password? The price of a gallon of gas? Your weight (before and after your diet)?

We have a remarkable, built-in capacity for memory, thank God.

If you can learn one single word, you can learn another. And if you learn two, you can learn four. The younger we are, the quicker our minds inscribe the data; but whatever our age, we should be actively practicing the discipline of Scripture memory.

This book is the result of a yearlong series of sermons I preached at my church on 100 Bible verses everyone on earth should know by heart. The week I began the series, one of my senior adults was rushed to the hospital with signs of a stroke. When I visited her the next day, she couldn't wait to tell me she was still intent on learning her verse for the week. "Oh, don't worry about me, Pastor," she said with effort. "I have my verse right here; I'm going to work on it while I'm in the hospital."

Another woman, eighty-nine years old, came up to me the next Sunday. "Oh, Pastor Morgan," she said. "I'm so glad you're having us memorize those verses. I've already gotten started on them. It's going to help me keep my mind fresh and young!"

While writing this book, I had lunch with Cliff Barrows, the music director for the Billy Graham Crusades. Cliff was influenced by the Navigators early in life and started memorizing verses as a young man. Now in his eighties, he told me he works every day on Scripture memory. Poor eyesight doesn't deter him. His wife, Ann, records passages on a handheld recorder, and Cliff listens to them over and over until he has them down pat.

Some books offer elaborate systems for memorizing material, but I only have ten tried-and-true suggestions.

First, make up your mind you can memorize just one verse. That's all. Just one. (Of course, if you can memorize one verse, you can memorize two.)

Second, work at it every day. Make it a simple part of your daily routine. It might be at the breakfast table, at the shaving mirror, in the drive-to-work traffic, while jogging, during your daily workout, at the end of your morning quiet time, during your evening bath, or just before you turn your light off at night. Let it piggyback on some other activity, the habit of which is already established, like your daily power walk.

Third, keep your current memory verse on whatever screens you use, such as your handheld phone or your computer screen. Post it on your refrigerator. Slide it under the glass of your desk or tape it to the dashboard of your car. Use sticky-notes everywhere. This is akin to the Bible's advice of writing it on the doorposts of your house and on the walls of your rooms.

Fourth, repeat, repeat, repeat. Say the verse aloud over and over. Whenever I conduct a wedding, I write out my comments and read the vows to the nervous couple unless I'm using the traditional ones I've used for years. Even those I still tack into my notes, but I seldom look down at them. I've said them so often I memorized them without realizing it.

In taking the woman I hold by the right hand to be my wedded wife, I promise to love her, honor her, and cherish her in this relationship, and, leaving all others, cleave only unto her in all things a true and faithful husband so long as we both shall live.

When I realized how I'd learned those words by sheer repetition, I decided the same could happen with Bible verses. So every morning during my devotions, I repeat a Bible verse aloud slowly, as if giving it to a bride and groom. In that way I'm gradually learning new verses, one by one. Repetition moves the verse from sensory memory to short-term memory, and from short-term memory to long-term storage, and from long-term storage to everyday use. In other words, first you have the verse, and then the verse has you.

My wife repeats her memory verses aloud, often using little songs she's composed for the words. She finds that singing a verse, even with a made-up tune, helps her remember it for years. (Of course, sometimes she can't quote the verse for others without singing it first.)

Sixth, read each verse in its context and study it. Write it out. Check out different translations, and memorize it in the translation you use the most.

Seventh, learn the reference as part of the verse.

Eighth, review, review, review.

Ninth, figure out some homemade mnemonics and mental associations, either for the verse or for the reference. I remember Proverbs 19:11 because my dad was born in 1911 and this verse reminds me of him: "A man's wisdom gives him patience; it is to his glory to overlook an offense" (NIV).

Tenth, use your verses. Preach them to yourself, quote them for others, and turn them into prayers to the Lord. Say with the psalmist: "Your word I have hidden in my heart, that I might not sin against You" (Ps. 119:11 NKJV).

It's as easy as that. Now let's get started on our first 100!

PART 2

100 VERSES EVERYONE SHOULD KNOW BY HEART

BEGINNINGS:

The Bible's Fantastic Four

1. Genesis 1:1

In the beginning God created the heavens and the earth.

Scripture begins with these ten words. This is the bedrock of the Bible, the first, earliest, and most irreducible foundation for the remaining thirty-one thousand verses of God's Word. Genesis 1:1 encompasses the totality of Truth. Without it there's nothing but despair. With it there's everything we need. If this verse is true, everything in the rest of the Bible is plausible and logically consistent. Genesis 1:1 tells us that God *is*, that He *creates*, and that He *speaks*; and this is the basis of all clear thinking and real hope.

Genesis 1:1 gives us roots. We're not accidental blobs of dying chemicals mysteriously evolving from primordial sludge without purpose or meaning. We have a past rooted in the glory of the God whose image we bear. We're wonderfully made and placed in an environment fine-tuned for our needs. The book of Genesis gives us the history of creation, sin, the beginnings of human society, and the wondrous plan of redemption introduced by God. If you discard Genesis 1:1, you abandon the roots and reality of humanity on earth. By removing this text from conscious thought, we lose all inherent moral law in the universe, all intrinsic bases for self-image, all eternal purpose to life, and any and all hope in the human heart.

Genesis 1:1 gives us routes. If we have a past, we have a future. If we were created in God's image, we have eternal potential. If we have an intelligent Creator who knows and loves us, He must have a purpose and plan for time and eternity. Without Him we're dying embers in a dying universe with no ultimate significance. With Him we have roots in a dignified past and routes to a great future.

Samuel Wesley, younger brother of John and Charles, was born February 10, 1690, but for about five years he didn't speak a word. Then one day he hid under a table while his mother, Susanna, looked for him. Finally he cried, "Here I am, mother." He had learned to talk! Susanna taught him to read, using Genesis 1:1, which he quickly memorized. Soon he had memorized Genesis 1:1–10. It's no wonder he later wrote this hymn: *Hail, Father, whose creating call Unnumbered worlds attend; Jehovah, comprehending all, Whom none can comprehend!*[16]

※ The Earth reminded us of a Christmas tree ornament hanging in the blackness of space. As we got farther and farther away it diminished in size. Finally it shrank to the size of a marble, the most beautiful marble you can imagine. That beautiful, warm, living object looked so fragile, so delicate, that if you touched it with a finger it would crumble and fall apart. Seeing this has to change a man, has to make a man appreciate the creation of God and the love of God.[17]—Astronaut James Irwin

2. John 1:1

In the beginning was the Word, and the Word was with God, and the Word was God.

There are two great mysteries at the heart of Christianity, the Trinity and the person of Jesus Christ: (1) God the three in one; and (2) Jesus the two in one. How could God be one God yet eternally exist in three distinct persons, and how can Jesus be one person yet possess two distinct natures, fully God and fully human?

This verse touches both mysteries. He (Christ, the Word) *was* God, yet He was *with* God in the beginning. He was God, yet distinct from God.

The great theme of John's Gospel is the divinity of Christ, and it reaches its climax in the declaration of Thomas in John 20:28: "My Lord and my God!" But the first verse, John 1:1, provides the backdrop for the whole book. Note the progression of logic in this verse:

- John 1:1 speaks of our Christ's preexistence: *In the beginning was the Word.*
- It also speaks of His coexistence: *And the Word was with God.*
- And John 1:1 speaks of His divine existence: *And the Word was God.*

The Trinity and Jesus! Both mysteries are imponderables we can never fathom, which is only to be expected if God is really God and Jesus is truly who He claims to be. It's been said that a God small enough to be understood isn't big enough to be worshipped. We need a transcendent God who boggles our minds with His immensity and who brings His infinities to bear on our infirmities. We need a gospel that opens with words like these: *In the beginning was the Word, and the Word was with God, and the Word was God.*

Georgia Gordon, who grew up in the deep South in the days of slavery, received no education as a young girl. But one day she heard a preacher reciting John 1:1. Deeply impressed, she memorized the verse; and when she got home, she asked someone who could read to point out the verse in the Bible. She studied it until she could recognize the words one by one, and she searched through the Bible for others like them. In this way, little by little, she learned to read. She later became a brilliant student at Fisk University in Nashville and one of the famous Jubilee Singers from Fisk who introduced Black Spirituals to the world.[18]

MEMORY TIP

Genesis 1:1 and John 1:1 have a similar chapter-and-verse "address," and they start with the same words. Genesis 1:1 focuses on God in the beginning and John 1:1 on Jesus—the Word—in the beginning. By memorizing them together, you're almost learning two verses as easily as one.

※ Here are two mysteries for the price of one—the plurality of persons within the unity of God, and the union of Godhead and manhood in the person of Christ. . . . The more you think about it, the more staggering it gets.[19]—J. I. Packer

3. John 1:14

The Word became flesh and took up residence among us.
We observed His glory, the glory as the One and Only
Son from the Father, full of grace and truth.

When was the last time you spent the night in a tent? It was last night. According to 2 Corinthians 5, we are currently living in the tents of our bodies, eagerly waiting resurrection day when we'll receive permanent structures (our glorified bodies). Furthermore, we're told in John 1:14 that when Jesus took on flesh in Bethlehem, He pitched His tent among us. The Greek term for "took up residence" has reference to tenting.

John 1:14 is arguably the Bible's greatest verse about the incarnation. The Word (God the Son) became flesh (human) and took up residence (pitched His tent) among us. We observed His glory and saw that He was the one and only God the Son, full of grace and truth.

The prologue of John (John 1:1–18) is one of the greatest introductions in the world of literature. The theme is Jesus, and the progression of thought is remarkable. In memorizing John 1:14, take time to study the entire passage, using this outline as a guide.

1. **Jesus is the God who made us** (1:1–3). He is God, existing from the beginning and through whom all things were made.
2. **He is the life who sustains us** (v. 4a). In Him was life!
3. **He is the light who illumines us** (vv. 4b–5). His life is our light. It shines in the darkness, and the darkness can't overcome it.
4. **He is the message who excites us** (vv. 6–9). John the Baptist testified about Him, and so can we.
5. **He is the Savior who redeems us** (vv. 10–13). All who receive Him and who believe in His name are given the right to become children of God.
6. **He is the friend who dwells among us** (v. 14). He pitched His tent here and tabernacles among us.

7. **He is the Lord who surpasses us** (v. 15). John the Baptist said of Him, "The One coming after me has surpassed me, because He existed before me."

8. **He is the Son who blesses us** (vv. 16–18). No one has ever seen God, but the one and only Son has revealed Him, and from the fullness of His grace we have all received one blessing after another (v. 16 NIV).

The word *incarnation* means "embodied in flesh." Dr. J. I. Packer wrote, "The incarnation is in itself an unfathomable mystery, but it makes sense of everything else that the New Testament contains." Packer points out that the reality of the incarnation pervades the Prologue of John. "The Church of England reads it annually as the Gospel for Christmas Day, and rightly so," said Packer. "Nowhere in the New Testament is the nature and meaning of Jesus' divine Sonship so clearly explained as here."[20]

✳ Jesus is God spelling Himself out in language that man can understand.[21]—Samuel D. Gordon

4. John 3:16

*For God loved the world in this way: He gave His One
and Only Son, so that everyone who believes in Him will
not perish but have eternal life.*

Henry Moorhouse, sixteen, was a gambler, gang leader, and thief.
But during the revival of 1859, he gave his life to Jesus and was soon
preaching the gospel with all his heart. His favorite text was John 3:16.
One day in 1867, in Ireland, he met the world evangelist D. L. Moody;
and Henry had the nerve to invite himself to preach in Moody's church
in Chicago.

Sometime later Moody returned home from a trip and learned that
Moorhouse had shown up, started preaching, and was drawing great
crowds. "He has preached two sermons from John 3:16," Moody's wife
told him, "and I think you will like him, although he preached a little
different from what you do."

"How is that?"

"Well, he tells sinners God loves them."

Moody wasn't so sure about that; but that evening he went to hear
Moorhouse preach. The young man stood up in the pulpit and said,
"If you will turn to the third chapter of John and the sixteenth verse,"
said the young man, "you will find my text." Moody later recalled, "He
preached a most extraordinary sermon from that verse. . . . I never knew
up to that time that God loved us so much. This heart of mine began to
thaw out, and I could not keep back the tears. It was like news from a far
country. I just drank it in."

Night after night Moorhouse preached from John 3:16, and it had
a life-changing effect on D. L. Moody. "I have never forgotten those
nights," Moody said later. "I have preached a different gospel since, and
I have had more power with God and man since then."

Later, when Moorhouse fell ill and was on his deathbed, he looked
up and told his friends, "If it were the Lord's will to raise me again,
I should like to preach from the text, 'God so loved the world.'"[22]

Notice that the word *gospel* is literally spelled out in this verse: "For **G**od loved the world in this way: He gave His **O**ne and **O**nly **S**on, so that everyone who believes in Him will not **P**erish but have **E**ternal **L**ife."

MEMORY TIP

When you've memorized Genesis 1:1; John 1:1; 1:14; and 3:16, you have the entire Bible in the palm of your hand. These verses are the four corners of God's Word.

※ My friends, for a whole week I have been trying to tell you how much God loves you, but I cannot do it with this poor stammering tongue. If I could borrow Jacob's ladder and climb up into heaven and ask Gabriel, who stands in the presence of the Almighty, to tell me how much love the Father has for the world, all he could say would be, "God so loved the world, that He gave His only begotten Son."—Henry Moorhouse

The Roman Road:

The Plan of Salvation

5. Romans 3:23

For all have sinned and fall short of the glory of God.

Our first four verses (Genesis 1:1; John 1:1, 14, and 3:16) give us the bare bones of biblical truth. The next five provide a comprehensive outline for God's plan of salvation.

The Bible is a big book—sixty-six divisions and more than thirty-one thousand verses—so the Lord placed a summary of it in the Scriptures, a digest, an abridgement, a prospectus. It's called the book of Romans, and it's a synopsis of the message of the entire Bible. Within Romans is a series of verses that give us an outline of God's entire plan of salvation for the human race. These verses are often called the Roman Road—Romans 3:23; 6:23; 5:8; and 10:9–10, and 13.

I don't know who first put these verses together and called them the Roman Road, but I know when I first became acquainted with them. I was a boy growing up in Elizabethton, Tennessee, and an evangelist came to hold a revival. I don't recall his name. He had a stamp and ink pad, and everywhere he went he stamped the Roman Road in the front of people's Bibles. I remember taking my Bible up to him after one of the services, and he pressed his stamp into the ink pad and then carefully transferred the verses to my Bible. As I recall, the stamp just said, "The Roman Road," and it listed the references for these verses.

In the years since, I've learned many methods of leading someone to Christ, but I find that I keep going back to this old series of verses because they summarize everything we need to tell others about how to receive Christ as Savior.

The first stop on this road is Romans 3:23. We have all sinned and fallen short of the perfect standards and holy expectations of the God of all glory. We are separated from Him by our sins. Before the good news of salvation, we have to know the bad news of sin.

Only three people in the history of the world have been perfect and sinless, and the first two didn't stay that way—Adam and Eve. That leaves only Jesus Himself. No one else can ever gain access into God's presence or eternal life on the basis of one's own perfections or righteous efforts. We have all sinned and have fallen short of the requirements of God's glory. We can never be reconciled to God by trying to live a good life, for we are intrinsically, internally sinful; and nothing sinful can exist in the blazing holiness of God's presence and perfections. Only when we realize this can we fully appreciate what Christ has done for us.

※ We can love our own, and also the good and the gracious; but God loves the ungodly, the worst of sinners and the most bitter blasphemers. Our part is to accept that love in His Son, our Savior.[23]
—V. Raymond Edman

6. Romans 6:23

For the wages of sin is death, but the gift of God is eternal life in Christ Jesus our Lord.

With the possible exception of John 3:16, no other text in Scripture better sums up all sixty-six books and thirty-one thousand verses of the Bible. This is the ultimate *Reader's Digest* version of God's Word. Notice the way the verse is balanced between its two clauses:

The wages of sin is death.
The gift of God is eternal life.

If we pull out the primary words of Romans 6:23 and place them side by side, we can see its logic and contrasting argument:

Wages—Gift
Sin—God
Death—Eternal Life

Wages is a word we see in our newspaper every day. It's what we get for what we do. The Bible says that we're all employed by sin, and the result or payback is physical, spiritual, and eternal death. In contrast to that, God wants to give us a gift, which is everlasting life.

It's a gift that only comes wrapped in one package—Jesus Christ our Lord! Think of a great canyon. We're on one side in a state of sin and death; God is on the other side with the gift of eternal life. The cross of Jesus Christ is the only bridge that spans the chasm. As 1 Timothy 2:5 says in *The Living Bible*: "God is on one side and all the people on the other side, and Christ Jesus, himself a man, is between them to bring them together."

When I preach, I sometimes turn to various passages, moving from one to the other in logical order. Using a pencil, I'll jot the next reference beside the prior one. In that way, if I forget which verse comes next, I have a reminder. We can do the same with the Roman Road. Beside Romans 3:23, pencil in the margin 6:23. Beside 6:23, pencil in 5:8; and beside that verse put 9:9–10. If you do this in a small, pocket-sized New Testament that you carry with you, you'll always be ready to lead someone to the facts they need to find eternal life in Jesus Christ.

MEMORY TIP

Write the references of the Roman Road in the front of your Bible, repeat the verses frequently, practice them on a buddy, and then ask God to bring someone across your path with whom you can share this simple, effective route to salvation in Christ:

The Roman Road

Romans 3:23 • Romans 6:23 • Romans 5:8 • Romans 10:9–10, 13

※ The Roman Road: This is one of the most effective presentations for people who've heard the message but need to see it in black and white, right out of the pages of the Bible. It's based on . . . verses in the book of Romans. I'd suggest highlighting these in your Bible so that they're easy to find and show to others.[24]—Bill Hybels

7. Romans 5:8

But God proves His own love for us in that while we were still sinners Christ died for us!

When Charles Evans Hughes, America's secretary of state in the 1920s, attended an important meeting of the Pan-American Conference, he gave his interpreter an unusual request. He wanted a summarized translation of what was being spoken in Spanish or Portuguese, but he added, "I want you to give me every word after the speaker says *but*."[25]

The word *but* is a conjunction that implies a sudden change of direction in the thought. And when we see this word in the Bible, it's important to understand every word that follows it, especially if the phrase is *but God . . . !*

- *But God* said, "No. Your wife Sarah will bear you a son." (Gen. 17:19)
- It was not you who sent me here, *but God*. (Gen. 45:8)
- I am about to die, *but God* . . . (Gen. 50:24)
- Do not be afraid or discouraged, . . . the battle is not yours, *but God*'s. (2 Chron. 20:15)
- *But God* was watching over the Jewish elders. (Ezra 5:5)
- *But* our *God* turned the curse into a blessing. (Neh. 13:2)
- *But God* will redeem my life from the power of Sheol. (Ps. 49:15)
- My flesh and my heart may fail, *but God* is the strength of my heart, my portion forever. (Ps. 73:26)
- *But God* was with him. (Acts 7:9)
- *But God* raised Him from the dead. (Acts 13:30)
- *But God* gave the growth. (1 Cor. 3:6)
- *But God*, who comforts the humble, comforted us. (2 Cor. 7:6)
- *But God*, who is abundant in mercy, because of His great love that He had for us, made us alive with the Messiah even though we were dead in trespasses. (Eph. 2:4–5)

Romans 5:8 is perhaps the greatest of all the "But God" statements in the Bible: But God proves His own love for us in that while we were still sinners Christ died for us!

MEMORY TIP

If we read and study a verse in its context, we can more easily memorize a verse and its reference. This verse is found in the middle of the paragraph in Romans 5 that runs from verse 6 to verse 11. The whole paragraph is worth memorizing, for it contains some of the richest verses in the Bible about the willingness of Jesus Christ to offer Himself for our sins. Read this paragraph repeatedly to understand the context for verse 8, and memorizing it will come much more naturally.

※ "Christ died for us." Here is a simple sentence in four words. The first two words state a historical fact: 'Christ died.' The second two add the theological significance: 'for us.' The full four form the crux of the Gospel: 'Christ died for us.' Never did four short words hold bigger or better message.[26]—J. Sidlow Baxter

8. Romans 10:9

*If you confess with your mouth, "Jesus is Lord," and
believe in your heart that God raised Him from the
dead, you will be saved.*

As a boy, I heard my dad talk about a favorite preacher of his, a
man named Hyman Appelman. Recently I came across a biography of
Dr. Appelman and discovered he was born into a Russian Jewish family
in 1902. When he was twelve, his family immigrated to America and
settled in Chicago where Appelman grew up to become a hardworking
attorney. In 1924, Appelman, suffering from a physical breakdown, traveled west to recover and checked into the downtown YMCA in Kansas
City. There he met a newspaper reporter who witnessed to him about
Jesus Christ. Later he began reading a Bible he found in his room.

Traveling to Denver, Appelman met other Christians, including a
local pastor who told him, "You don't need a doctor, my boy; you need
the Lord Jesus Christ!" The pastor opened a Bible to Romans 10:9 and
explained the verse as carefully as he knew how. Appelman, 23, prayed
and claimed this text as his own. But when he sent a telegram to tell
his family what he'd done, they were horrified. His fiancée broke the
engagement, and Appelman was an outcast from his friends. He perse-
vered through difficult days and went on to become one of the greatest
evangelists of his era. Hundreds of thousands of people confessed Christ
in his meetings, and he often referred to himself as "a little Jew with a
big Jesus."

The phrase "Jesus is Lord" was the New Testament confession of
faith. It is the acknowledgment that Jesus Christ is God Himself and
that we are making Him the Lord of our lives. This is our declaration
when we decide to believe and receive the truth of the risen Christ. If you
confess with your mouth, "Jesus is Lord," and believe in your heart that
God raised Him from the dead, you will be saved. For with your heart
you believe and are justified, and with your mouth that you confess and
are saved.

MEMORY TIP

We can't memorize everything, and there's no reason to learn use-less information. We must be intentional about what we memorize. In her book *Total Recall,* Joan Minninger says, "Scientists estimate that we remember only 1 out of every 100 pieces (of information) we receive. If we remembered everything, they say, we would be 'paralyzed by infor-mation overload.' A good memory must be selective."[27] As intentional memorizers, let's select key Scriptures and deliberately inscribe them on the walls of our brains.

※ The remedy is not only the gospel of the Lord Jesus Christ, but the gospel of the Lord Jesus Christ preached in the power and demonstra-tion of the Holy Spirit. It is the gospel preached ceaselessly, endlessly, the gospel planted beside all waters, the gospel pressed andimpressed upon the hearts of the multitudes.[28]—Hyman Appelman

9. Romans 10:10

With the heart one believes, resulting in righteousness,
and with the mouth one confesses, resulting in salvation.

In his book *Scripture Memory for Successful Soul-Winning,* Oscar Lowry confesses that when he began training for Christian ministry, he had an undisciplined mind. He didn't believe he could memorize verses so he filled the flyleaf of his Bible with references helpful for counseling. When talking with others, he'd turn to the front of his Bible, find a suitable passage, then look it up, and read it. This was a workable plan but not the best one.

Lowry finally determined, "If I can memorize one verse, then I can memorize one more, and ten more, and even one hundred." Rising early the next morning, he chose Romans 10:9–10, even though it seemed to him like a difficult place to start. He paced across his room, repeating these verses, muttering them over, trying to hammer them into his head. "I will do this thing," he told himself, and within a half hour he had the verses memorized.

The next morning he reviewed Romans 10:9–10, then memorized another verse. He kept adding a new verse every morning while diligently reviewing the prior ones. Months later it dawned on him he could repeat a hundred verses without looking at his Bible, and that the work was becoming easier as his brain adjusted to its new patterns of memorization.

By the time of his death, Lowry had learned more than twenty thousand verses, about two-thirds of the Bible, and could locate each with chapter and verse. It all began with Romans 10:9–10.[29]

In memorizing Romans 10:9–10, notice that both verses speak of twin actions that enable us to claim salvation. We believe with our hearts and confess with our mouths. But the order is reversed in the two verses. Verse 9 tells us to confess with our mouth and to believe in our hearts. Verse 10 explains that we believe with our hearts and confess with our mouths. That's not a contradiction; it's a mirror image of the process. Quote verse 9, and then learn verse 10 as if looking at verse 9 in a mirror. Scholars call this an A-B-B-A format. Verse 9 gives us the order from the outside in, and verse 10 gives us the order from the inside out. The two actions happen at once as we believe in our hearts that Jesus has risen from the dead; therefore we acknowledge that Jesus is Lord. Add verse 13, and you've mastered the entire "Roman Road."

※ It takes only a few brief words to enter the married life; but it will take thousands of confessions of love through word and act to live the married life. We enter the Christian life by faith in Christ and by confessing Him as Lord and Master of our lives; but it takes all the remaining days of our lives, our confessions of Him as Lord by our words and by the deeds of our lives, to live the Christian life.[30]—A. B. Kendall

LISTENING:

The Word of God and Prayer

10. 2 Timothy 3:16

All Scripture is inspired by God and is profitable for teaching, for rebuking, for correcting, for training in righteousness.

The Bible is chock-full of verses attesting to its inspiration, authority, infallibility, and usefulness. Perhaps the best New Testament texts on this subject are 2 Timothy 3:16 and 2 Peter 1:21. The latter says, in effect, that no passage in the Bible came about by a prophet's own origination, but the writers of Scripture spoke as they were moved (borne along) by the Holy Spirit. The former verse tells us that all Scripture is inspired (breathed out) by God and therefore of immense usefulness in our lives.

Notice the chapter/verse location 2 Timothy 3:16. There's a remarkable correspondence between John 3:16 and 2 Timothy 3:16. The two verses have more in common than their "street address" of 316.

- John 3:16 talks about the Savior, and 2 Timothy 3:16 talks about the Scriptures. These two entities comprise the two greatest gifts ever bestowed on humanity.
- Both are called "The Word."
- One is the living Word, and the other is the written Word.

- Both are utterly unique. Jesus is like no other person the world has ever seen, and the Bible is like no other book the world has ever read.
- Jesus was both fully human and fully divine. He came down from heaven yet made His appearance through the instrumentality of a human being who was overshadowed by the Holy Spirit. The Scriptures are both fully human and fully divine. They came down from heaven yet were given through the instrumentality of human beings who were borne along by the Holy Spirit.
- Just as the Savior was without sin, the Scriptures are without error.
- Just as the Savior has a dual nature, the Scriptures have a double nature.
- The Savior is the God-Man, and the Scriptures are from both God and man.
- The Savior came to save us, and the Scriptures were given to tell us how to be saved.
- The Bible is Jesus in print, and Jesus is the personification and fulfillment of the Scriptures. And so these 3:16s are twin verses about the Savior and the Scriptures.

The Great "3:16s" of the New Testament

- Luke 3:16—The Baptism of the Holy Spirit
- 1 Corinthians 3:16—The Holy Spirit's Indwelling
- Ephesians 3:16—The Holy Spirit's Strengthening
- Colossians 3:16—The Imbedded Word
- 2 Thessalonians 3:16—The All-Encompassing Peace of God
- 1 Timothy 3:16—The Uniqueness of Christ
- 1 John 3:16—The Power of Love
- Revelation 3:16—The Danger of Lukewarm Love

✳ Inspiration . . . is the determining influence exercised by the Holy Spirit on the writers of the Old and New Testament in order that they might proclaim and set down in an exact and authentic way the message as received from God.[31]—René Pache

11. Joshua 1:8

*This book of instruction must not depart from your
mouth; you are to recite it day and night, so that you
may carefully observe everything written in it. For then
you will prosper and succeed in whatever you do.*

"I recall and repeat often now the first Scripture passage I ever
memorized," wrote evangelist Arthur Flake in his book *Life at Eighty as
I See It.* He was referring to Joshua 1:8. "I memorized this more than fifty
years ago. It is still fresh and invigorating, and I love it."[32]

I, too, have a clear recollection of memorizing this verse. I was
attending a small Navigator Discipleship Bible Study in my college dormitory. When this verse was assigned for memorizing, I thought it too
long and cumbersome. But it finally worked its way into my long-term
memory, and it's never left.

It contains a threefold command: (1) This book of the law must not
depart from your mouth. We must keep speaking it, reading it, repeating
it, hearing it. (2) We're to meditate on God's Word day and night. The
original Hebrew word came from a verb meaning "to mutter," as if muttering to yourself. We're to let verses of Scripture roll around in our minds
all the time. We meditate on something by memorizing, visualizing, and
personalizing it. We mutter it around in our minds by day and go to sleep
at night letting its words sink into our subconscious. (3) Having read and
meditated on God's Word, we put it into practice and obey it.

Joshua 1:8 ends with a twofold promise: (1) If we read, meditate,
and obey God's law, we will prosper; and (2) we will succeed in whatever
we do. As we meditate on God's Word, our minds are improved. They
are God conditioned. We begin thinking more as He thinks, looking
at life from His point of view. As we're transformed by the renewing of
our thoughts, we become successful in those things God appoints for us
to do.[33]

Take time to read Psalm 1 in light of Joshua 1:8. Perhaps you'll agree with me that King David took Joshua 1:8 and did what it said, meditating on it, visualizing it, and personalizing it, using the image of trees planted by rivers of water. From that meditation he wrote Psalm 1. In other words, David showed us how to do it! Psalm 1 is his meditation about meditating on Joshua 1:8.

✳ Meditation is the skeleton key that unlocks the greatest storeroom in the house of God's provision for the Christian. . . . [It is] holding the Word of God in your heart until it has affected every phase of your life . . . . Beware of getting alone with your own thoughts. Get alone with God's thoughts. There is danger in rummaging through waste and barren desert-thoughts that can be labeled—daydreaming or worse. Don't meditate upon yourself but dwell upon God. . . . Make this a built-in habit of daily living.[34]—From a Navigator's booklet

12. Psalm 119:11

*I have treasured Your word in my heart so that I may
not sin against You.*

My first pastorate was a little stone church in the Tennessee hills.
One day in Sunday school, an old woman stood and quoted Psalm 119
from memory, word for word, all 176 verses. This is the longest chapter
in the Bible. She had learned it in childhood, and it had enriched her
throughout her life.

Psalm 119 is longer than some entire books of the Bible, yet remark-
ably it was written to be memorized. It's divided into twenty-two stanzas
of eight verses each, following the twenty-two letters of the Hebrew
alphabet. To put it simply, every verse in the first stanza begins with the
Hebrew equivalent of the English letter A, and so on until we come to
the last stanza (vv. 169–176), which ends with the last letter of the
Hebrew alphabet. This served as a built-in memory device to enable
Hebrew children to learn the whole passage by heart.

Furthermore, virtually every verse of Psalm 119 has to do with the
Word of God.

Psalm 119:11 promises that if we hide God's Word in our hearts, it
will retard the development of sin in our lives. All of us are tempted in
different ways, but there are verses in the Bible to equip us to fight whatever temptation we face.

- When lured by addictive tendencies, try memorizing portions
  of Romans 6.
- When tempted by greed, find help in 1 Timothy 6.
- When tempted to be anxious or depressed, Philippians 4 can
  rescue you.
- When you feel lazy, bored, or lonely, verses in Romans 12 are
  at your disposal.
- When facing anger and bitterness, memorize verses at the end
  of Ephesians 4.

- When facing sexual temptation, the first part of Ephesians 5 can be a big help.

When Jesus was tempted by the devil, He quoted memorized Scripture, giving us an example. If we'll fill our minds with God's Word, we'll have the weapons needed to fend off the attacks of the evil one. God has put more than thirty-one thousand verses in this Book to help us withstand the temptations we face in life. It's like having thirty-one thousand rounds of ammunition; and there's no excuse for having your arsenal empty.

In olden England, when metrical psalms were sung instead of hymns, it took congregations quite a while to sing all the way through Psalm 119. According to one account, Rev. William Grimshaw of Haworth would sometimes announce the singing of Psalm 119 while he left the building and walked through the village looking for truant worshippers. He had plenty of time to round up the slackers and herd them into church before the psalm was over; then he would preach to them. It was said absentees were more frightened of Grimshaw than of the justice of the peace.[35]

※ Sin will keep us from the Bible, or the Bible will keep us from sin. —attributed to D. L. Moody

13. Deuteronomy 6:6

*These words that I am giving you today are to be in your
heart.*

I've been alarmed by a recent series of surveys showing the rapidity of
spiritual decline in the Western world. Only 35 percent of American congregations now describe themselves as spiritually vital and alive. Southern
Baptists say that if current trends continue in their denomination, their
churches will be reduced in half by 2050. In England the Anglicans
expect to decline by 90 percent by 2050. Other surveys have found the
percentage of people claiming no religion has risen in every state in
America, and the number of Americans who claim to be Christians is
rapidly decreasing. Headlines warn of the "coming collapse of evangelical
Christianity in America."

The most alarming statistics involve teenagers and young adults.
Masses of them are leaving the church after high school, and only a percentage of them return in a regular, sustained way.

I believe Deuteronomy 6:4–9 is the most vital parenting passage in
the Bible. If followed, it has the power to reverse those statistics. This
passage gives three golden rules for rearing children:

1. **Love the Lord your God with all your heart, soul, and
    strength.** The single most powerful influence in a child's life
    is his or her parents' visible, passionate love for the Lord Jesus
    Christ (Deut. 6:4–5).

2. **His Word must be on your heart.** We must love God's
    Word and read it daily. It's more important than newspapers,
    newscasts, sports, or hobbies. Our children should see us
    pouring over God's Word every morning or evening
    (Deut. 6:6).

3. **We must share with our children spontaneously and
    naturally any verses God gives us.** Speak about them when
    we sit at home, drive down the road, lie down at night, and
    get up in the morning. When the natural conversations of

the home are sprinkled with God's Word, it's like constantly planting seeds in the fertile hearts of our youngsters (Deut. 6:7–9)

MEMORY TIP

I have friends who call this passage *D6*. They want churches to become D6 churches and parents D6 parents when it comes to sharing God's Word with their children. If you get this letter-number coded in your mind, D6, you'll never have any trouble locating this vital passage in the Bible.

※ Each morning when I went downstairs to breakfast, my father—a busy missionary surgeon—would be sitting reading his Bible. At night, her work behind her, my mother would be doing the same. Anything that could so capture the interest and devotion of those I admired and loved the most, I reasoned, must be worth investigating. So at an early age I began reading my Bible and found it to be, in the words of the old Scotsman, "sweet pasturage."[36]—Ruth Bell Graham

14. Deuteronomy 6:7

*Repeat them to your children. Talk about them when
you sit in your house and when you walk along the road,
when you lie down and when you get up.*

I read an interesting book about the French impressionist Edouard Manet and gained an insight about small blessings like flower blossoms, special moments, and Bible verses. Manet often became dissatisfied with his larger paintings, and he would destroy the canvas by slicing out small scenes with which he was pleased and which seemed good enough to stand by themselves. These small cutouts became masterpieces. A good example is *Women at the Races*, which is now displayed at the Cincinnati Art Museum. It was originally part of a large painting, but Manet deemed it the only part of the scene worth saving so he cut it out. The smaller painting (about seventeen by thirteen inches) is a wonder in itself.

We love all of the Word of God, but sometimes just a small verse cut from the Bible thrills our hearts. We're grateful for long volumes of interesting literature, but sometimes just a Scripture phrase can encourage us. Thank God for the miniatures of His grace!

In Deuteronomy 6 we're told that the most effective "family altars" occur frequently, spontaneously, and naturally through the day as we share these "miniatures" with our children. I remember once when my father pulled me aside to show me a verse in the book of Amos that was fascinating to him. It fascinated me, too.

I know of a mother whose child suffered bad dreams at night. "Let me show you this Bible verse, which has helped me," she said, opening to Psalm 4:8. The child memorized the verse, and his nighttime fears evaporated.

Dwight Eisenhower once told of a boyhood episode of losing his temper and storming to his room in a rage. After while, his mother came in and showed him Proverbs 16:32: "Patience is better than power, and controlling one's temper, than capturing a city." It was a lesson Ike never forgot, which later served him well as supreme Allied commander during World War II and as president of the United States.

Little verses, little truths, little insights, shared spontaneously, memorized in the family circle—this is the most powerful technique we have in raising our children in the fear and nurture of the Lord.

✳ Have you ever noticed this? Whatever need or trouble you are in, there is always something to help you in your Bible, if only you go on reading till you come to the word God specially has for you. I have noticed this often. Sometimes the special word is in the portion you would naturally read, or in the Psalms for the day, or in *Daily Light*, or maybe it is somewhere else; but you must go on till you find it, for it is always somewhere. You will know it the moment you come to it, and it will rest your heart.[37]—Amy Carmichael

15. Hebrews 4:12

*For the word of God is living and effective and sharper
than any two-edged sword, penetrating as far as to
divide soul, spirit, joints, and marrow; it is a judge of the
ideas and thoughts of the heart.*

Yes, this verse is a little longer and more complicated than some we're learning, but it can be easily memorized by understanding its progression and by taking it one phrase at a time.

Context: Read through Hebrews 3:7–4:12, underlining every one of the twelve occurrences of the word "rest." God wanted to give the Israelites rest (abiding security and peace) in the promised land, but they didn't trust Him. Their hearts were hardened in unbelief. Likewise, God wants to give us abiding security and peace, both now (spiritually) and in heaven (eternally). But we must take Him seriously at His word, not spurning or doubting it. The writer says, "Let us then make every effort to enter that rest, so that no one will fall into the same pattern of disobedience. For the word of God is living and effective" (Heb. 4:11–12).

Characteristics: The Word of God is: (1) living—not dead, archaic, or irrelevant; and it is (2) effective. The Greek word here is *energēs*, from which we get our word *energy*. The Bible is high-voltage. It has the unlimited energy of God behind it and will not return to Him void (Isa. 55:11).

Cutting: The Word of God is a double-edged sword. Some commentators believe this image is based on the knives the Levitical priests used to cut through the deepest sections of the sacrificial animals. Wielded by our great high priest, God's Word penetrates to the depths of our hearts and souls. No part of our personality is unaffected by Scripture as we hear and respond to it.

Criticizing: The Scriptures judge the thoughts and intents of the heart. The word *judge* is translated from the Greek word *kririkos,* from which we get our word *critic*. The Bible is the critic of the heart, pointing out weakness and showing us where to improve.

Don't get discouraged memorizing this verse. Work on it a step at a time as it unfolds in logic and memory. This is one of the great verses *in* God's Word *about* God's Word.

The Bible is like: a lamp to our feet (Ps. 119:105); bread for the soul (Matt. 4:4); a hammer that shatters the rock (Jer. 23:29); honey in the comb (Ps. 19:9–10); rain and snow that water the earth (Isa. 55:10–11); gold that enriches us (Ps. 19:9–10), fire that warms or burns us (Jer. 23:29); seed planted in the heart (Luke 8:11); water for washing (Eph. 5:26); a mirror for seeing and correcting ourselves (James 1:22–25); nourishing milk and meat for the soul (Heb. 5:12–13); and a double-edged sword (Heb. 4:12).

※ The Word of Christ proves itself to be the Word of God by its living energy and its penetrating power.[38]—A. T. Pierson

16. Hebrews 4:16

> *Therefore let us approach the throne of grace with bold-*
> *ness, so that we may receive mercy and find grace to help*
> *us at the proper time.*

This wonderful verse gives us the *who, what, where, why,* and *when* of prayer.

Who? *Let us* . . . The exhortation of Hebrews 4:16 has your name on it. The context reminds us that Jesus, our great high priest, has gone through the heavens before us, sympathizing with our weaknesses. He opens the door into the throne room of the universe for us.

What? Prayer is approaching God. *Therefore let us approach . . .* It is drawing near. James 4:8 tells us to draw near to God, and Deuteronomy 4:7 tells us how by asking who else has a god as near to them "as the LORD our God is to us, whenever we call to Him?" The chief purpose of prayer is recognizing the nearness of our King.

Where? *Let us approach the throne of grace.* It is a *throne,* a majestic and glorious seat of power. It's a throne of *grace,* not of judgment or condemnation. Through Christ we approach the throne of One who is our Friend, who desires fellowship with us, who wants to bless us from the endless resources of His grace.

Why? *So we may receive mercy and find grace to help us.* Mercy is God's attitude of forgiveness in not giving us what we *do* deserve. Grace is His attitude of blessing and benevolence in giving us what we *do not* deserve.

When? *At the proper time.* That phrase literally means at the opportune or needed time, just when we need it.

"I am never tired of pointing out that the Greek phrase translated, 'In the time of need,' is a colloquialism, of which 'the nick of time' is the exact equivalent: That we may have grace to help in the 'nick of time.' Grace just when and where I need it. You are attacked by temptation, and, at the moment of assault, you look to Him, and the grace is there to help in the nick of time. No postponement of your petition until the evening hour of prayer; but there . . . in the city street, with the flaming temptation in front of you, turn to Christ with a cry for help, and the grace will be there in the nick of time."[39]—G. Campbell Morgan

※ One day I was in trouble and oppressed about many things. It was one of those days when everything seems to go wrong. I was trying to get my Quiet time but was constantly interrupted. Suddenly these words came—I could hardly believe they were in the Bible, they seemed so new to my needy heart—"Grace to help in time of need." I found them and read them and marked them with joy, and in that moment, the moment of their coming, I was renewed in strength.[40] —Amy Carmichael

17. 1 John 5:14

*Now this is the confidence we have before Him: when-
ever we ask anything according to His will, He hears us.*

This verse and the next offer one of the Bible's best definitions of
prayer. It's easy to memorize when you notice how the verses unfold and
expand. The meaning and marvel of prayer grows deeper and more practical as phrase builds upon phrase. Prayer is . . .

- Coming before Him.
- Coming before Him with confidence.
- Coming before Him with confidence and asking.
- Coming before Him with confidence and asking according
  to His will.
- Coming before Him with confidence and asking according
  to His will, knowing that He hears us.

Writing near the end of the Bible and at the end of the apostolic
age, the apostle John wanted us to know something about the biblical
promises related to prayer. They are all conditioned by God's will. In
his Gospel, for example, John quoted Jesus as saying, "You may ask me
for anything in my name, and I will do it" (John 14:14 NIV). *Anything* is
a huge word, and perhaps some of John's readers had taken it a bit too
literally. So in 1 John 5:14, he reminds us that the promise of answered
prayer is dependent on the phrase "according to His will."

From the perspective of infinity, our God knows what's best from
beginning to end. He sees the outcomes of every chain reaction in life.
He knows how the dominoes fall and how the cookies crumble. His perfect, providential oversight makes no mistakes and always results in the
best for His children.

Our vantage point is as limited as a person who's fallen into a hole
and can only see a circle of sky above him. We don't always know the
landscape, and we can't see distant vistas. So we pray earnestly and ask
God for our needs, our wants, our wishes, and our desires. But we always

pray with the attitude, "if it be Your will." In that we can have total confidence.

Sometimes when I purchase roses or plants from a nursery catalog, there's a little box on the order form saying, "If we are out of the item you want, may we substitute one of equal or greater value?" I always say no, because I don't think the workers in the warehouse know what's best for my garden. But with the Lord we should always say, "Yes, Lord! You may substitute. You may grant an alternative answer of equal or greater value. I trust You with substitutions."

❋ The purpose of prayer is to get God's will done. . . . The greatest prayer any one can offer is "Thy will be done." It will be offered in a thousand different forms, with a thousand details, as needs arise daily. But every true prayer comes under those four words.[41]—S. D. Gordon

18. 1 John 5:15

And if we know that He hears whatever we ask, we
know that we have what we have asked Him for.

The Bible is full of facts about prayer; it's the world's greatest textbook on the subject. Here, near the end of Scripture, are two verses that seem to sum up the subject—1 John 5:14–15. Notice the sustained repetition that drives this passage into our hearts.

- This is the confidence . . . we know . . . we know.
- Whenever we ask . . . whatever we ask.
- Anything according to His will.
- He hears . . . He hears . . . we have.

Archbishop Trench said, "We must not conceive of prayer as an overcoming of God's reluctance but as a laying hold of His highest willingness." It's great to pray spontaneously throughout the day, before meetings, at stressful times, prior to responding in tense situations. But we need a regular time each morning and/or evening for a daily scheduled appointment with God. There we praise Him, confess our sins to Him, and bring to Him our needs. God often says yes to our requests. Sometimes it's no or wait. But this is our confidence: *He hears. . . . He hears. . . . We know. . . . We have.*

When God Says No

- Abraham earnestly prayed that Ishmael would become the son of promise and the heir of his legacy, but God said no. He had something better, a line of descent through the boy Isaac.
- Moses earnestly prayed to cross the river Jordan with the children of Israel, but God said no. He had a younger leader named Joshua and a better promised land for the aged Moses.
- David prayed earnestly for the joy of building a temple to the Lord, but God said no. He had something better—for David to plan the project and for his son Solomon to do the work.

- Jonah prayed earnestly that he would die, but God said no. He had something better—for Jonah to learn the lessons of compassion and write it down in a book that would thrill the ages.
- The healed demonic in Mark 5 prayed that he could travel around as a disciple of Jesus of Nazareth, but the Lord said no. He had something better—that he go home to his friends and tell them what great things the Lord had done for him and had shown him mercy.
- The apostle Paul prayed earnestly to be healed from his disease, which he described as a thorn in the flesh. But God said no. He had something better—for Paul to discover the all-sufficiency of His grace.
- Jesus prayed earnestly that the cup of suffering would pass from Him, but God said no. He had something better—that a fountain would be opened for all the world for the forgiveness of sin.

※ I never prayed sincerely for anything, but it came, at some time . . . somehow, in some shape.—Adoniram Judson

ASSURANCE:
Inner Peace and Security

19. 1 John 5:11

> *And this is the testimony: God has given us eternal life,*
> *and this life is in His Son.*

As a college sophomore, I was mentored by an upperclassman who gave me these two verses, 1 John 5:11–12, to memorize. He called them two of the best verses in the Bible about assurance of salvation. As long as I knew these verses, he said, I'd never doubt being saved. I've come back to them many times, and I'm thankful for what's *not* in them. There is no *maybe, if, might,* or *hope so . . .*

This is the testimony. This is what God Himself has declared as truth. This is the record. These are the facts.

He has . . . It's already done. This has been irrevocably accomplished.

He has given us . . . It's not just a generic promise that *He has given eternal life.* It includes that personal pronoun *us.* And *us* includes *you* and *me.*

He has given us eternal life. While the whole Bible teaches that God is eternal and He bestows everlasting life on His children, it's John who is the apostle of eternal life. He used the phrase twenty-three times in His writing.

And this life is in His Son. Jesus not only gives us life; He is the Source and Creator of life. And yet—paradox of the ages—He died to conquer death, and because He lives, we live also.

John on Eternal Life

- Everyone who believes on Him will not perish but have *eternal life.* (John 3:16)
- The one who believes in the Son has *eternal life.* (John 3:36)
- Anyone who hears My word and believes Him who sent Me has *eternal life.* (John 5:24)
- I assure you: Anyone who believes has *eternal life.* (John 6:47)
- Lord, who will we go to? You have the words of *eternal life.* (John 6:68)
- I gave them *eternal life,* and they will never perish. (John 10:28)
- This is *eternal life*: that they may know You, the only true God, and the One You have sent—Jesus Christ. (John 17:3)
- We . . . declare to you the *eternal life.* (1 John 1:2)
- And this is the promise that He Himself made to us: *eternal life.* (1 John 2:25)
- And this is the testimony: God has given us *eternal life,* and this life is in His Son. (1 John 5:11)
- I have written these things to you who believe in the name of the Son of God, so that you may know that you have *eternal life.* (1 John 5:13)

※ Our hope is not hung upon such an untwisted thread as, "I imagine so," or "It is likely," but the cable, the strong tow of our fastened anchor, is the oath and promise of Him who is eternal verity. Our salvation is fastened with God's own hand, and with Christ's own strength, to the strong stake of God's unchangeable nature.[42]—Samuel Rutherford

20. 1 John 5:12

The one who has the Son has life. The one who doesn't
have the Son of God does not have life.

Writing in a Gideon publication, Garry O. Parker recalled an exciting day when he was in the sixth grade. Several visitors were passing out a
special gift. As each class was called to the assembly room, these Gideons
gave a New Testament to every child who promised to read it. Garry
raised his hand and received his copy.

A few months later his mother passed away after a long illness, and
the following years were unsettled and difficult. One February night in
1957, Garry was sitting in his room reading his New Testament. He came
to 1 John 5:12: *The one who has the Son has life. The one who doesn't have*
the Son of God does not have life.

He saw clearly that our eternal future depends on whether we have
Jesus as our Savior and Lord, and that message pricked his heart like a
needle. "In that moment," Garry recalled, "God awakened my understanding, and I quietly put my trust in Jesus Christ as my personal Savior
and Lord. It was not an overly emotional moment but one of quiet certainty. It was the beginning of an adventure in faith with Jesus Christ,
which has continued to be exciting every day."

Garry became an effective pastor and now, retired, continues serving
the Lord with this message: *This is the testimony: God has given us eternal*
life, and this life is in His Son. The One who has the Son has life. The one
who doesn't have the Son of God does not have life.[43]

Great Assurance-of-Salvation Verses in the Bible

- I am persuaded that neither death nor life, nor angels nor rulers, nor things present, nor things to come, nor powers, nor height, nor depth, nor any other created thing will have the power to separate us from the love of God that is in Christ Jesus our Lord! (Rom. 8:38–39)
- I know whom I have believed and am persuaded that He is able to guard what has been entrusted to Him until that day. (2 Tim. 1:12)
- I give them eternal life, and they will never perish—ever! No one will snatch them out of My hand. . . . No one is able to snatch them out of the Father's hand. (John 10:28–29)

MEMORY TIP

The full 100 verses in this book include: (1) 1 John 5:11–12 about assurance of salvation; (2) and 1 John 5:14–15 about assurance of answered prayer. Why not memorize verse 13, too, and you'll have an entire paragraph of assurance packed away forever in your mind.

❊ The assurance of salvation is plainly written over the pages of the New Testament. Christ and His apostles lived in the air of certainty. . . . The epistles glow with the truth that we may know we possess salvation.[44]—Herbert Lockyer

21. John 14:1

*Your heart must not be troubled. Believe in God; believe
also in Me.*

To feel the impact of John 14:1, you have to read the end of the previous chapter, remembering there were no chapter breaks originally. This is part of the upper room discourse (John 13–17), as Jesus meets the final time with His disciples prior to His crucifixion. At the end of chapter 13, Jesus distressed His disciples by abruptly telling them He was leaving. He was going away and wouldn't be with them much longer.

"Lord," Simon Peter said to Him, "where are You going?"

Jesus answered, "Where I am going you cannot follow Me now, but you will follow later."

"Why can't I follow You now? I will lay down my life for You!"

"Will you lay down your life for me?" said Jesus. "I assure you: A rooster will not crow until you have denied Me three times."

There must have been a deathly pause in the conversation, but a moment later Jesus added: "Your heart must not be troubled. Believe in God; believe also in Me."

It's important to see this context because it shows us that the truths of John 14 work in the most troubling times of life. These words weren't spoken in the green pastures of Galilee on a cloudless spring day. They were spoken in a sealed room in a hostile city during a crisis in the face of impending doom. That's why we know it's able to reassure us, too, in life's deepest valleys, darkest days, and strangest twists and turns. We trust in God and in God's Son!

Eric Betz tells the story that while he grew up believing in God, nothing in his life demonstrated it. He occasionally attended church, but it was a chore. He was preoccupied with his family and pals, his job, and his girlfriend. Then in his late twenties everything fell apart. His parents separated, his friends moved away, he lost his job, and he and his fiancée split up. "At that point in my life, I lost all hope," said Eric. "I experienced many sleepless nights because of anxiety and depression. I was looking for inner peace."

Then one August day Eric found a pocket-sized Gideon New Testament in his apartment. Opening it, he found a page that said *Where to Find Help, When* . . . His eye fell on the reference for John 14:1, and he quickly searched through the pages for that verse. He read the entire paragraph, and suddenly his depression and anxiety faded. "I confessed to the Lord that I was a sinner and needed a Savior and asked Jesus to come into my life." He instantly discovered a gift of inner peace that matched the words of Jesus: *Your heart must not be troubled. Believe in God; believe also in Me.*[45]

✳ There is no trouble to which the heart of man is exposed that a belief in the doctrine of the Gospel is not calculated to purify and to alleviate.[46]—Thomas Chalmers

22. John 14:2

*In my Father's house are many dwelling places; if not,
I would have told you. I am going away to prepare a
place for you.*

Perhaps you're familiar with this verse from the King James Version: "In my Father's house are many mansions." It's among the most precious verses in the Bible about heaven; but modern translations have replaced the word *mansions* with "rooms" or "dwelling places."

I'm not happy that my heavenly accommodations have been downgraded from a mansion to a room. What gives?

Well, our English word *mansion* comes from a Latin word meaning "to live or dwell." Originally the word simply meant "a place to live or a place to dwell." When William Tyndale first translated the Bible into English, he used the word *manse* or *mansion*; it simply meant "dwelling place." From there it came into our early English versions. That was also the meaning of the Greek word used by John, and it fits the analogy Jesus is using about His Father's *house*.

But that doesn't mean we're all going to be confined to one-room efficiencies in some sort of heavenly tenement house throughout eternity. I actually think the word *mansion* is a pretty good one. After all, the smallest house in heaven is going to be a million times better than the grandest palace on earth, so I don't think the idea of *mansion* is inappropriate. I'm going to stick to my old King James terminology here. In my Father's house are many mansions.

What we often call heaven is referred to in Revelation 21 and 22 as the new heavens, the new earth, and the new Jerusalem. I'm convinced the Bible teaches that a literal city, new Jerusalem, is currently in the highest heaven and is the dwelling place of God. Christians are transported there instantly at death. At the end of earth's history, this world and the entire universe will be recreated. This glorious, golden city will then descend from the heaven to the new earth, and the dwelling place of God will be with us, and we will be His people, and He will be our God. Our eternal home will be on the new earth and in this great city. There'll be more than enough room for all the mansions, apartments, cottages, and dwelling places we'll ever need. In his book *Heaven,* Randy Alcorn writes, "Heaven isn't likely to have lots of identical residences. God loves diversity, and He tailor-makes His children *and* His provisions for them. When we see the particular place He's prepared for us—not just for mankind in general but for us in particular—we'll rejoice to see our ideal home."[47]

※ A tent or a cottage, why should I care? They're building a palace for me over there.—Harriet E. Buell

23. John 14:3

If I go away and prepare a place for you, I will come back and receive you to Myself, so that where I am you may be also.

When we were first married, my wife and I had a visit from a salesman who, wanting to sell us waterless cookware, offered to cook our supper one night. He pulled a pot from his suitcase, put in some carrots, and poured in a little water.

"I thought you said it was waterless," I said.

He replied: "It is. You use *less* water. It isn't water-*free*; it is water-*less*. Instead of boiling your vegetables in a quart of water and washing away the vitamins, you use just a few spoonfuls of water."

I wish I could say Christians can live a worry-*free* life; but by all means we must at least live a worry-*less* life. It's true that the Bible tells us not to worry or to let our hearts be troubled, but the fact that we're told *not* to worry implies the existence of worry in the life of the Christian.

Certainly in the upper room the disciples had reason to worry. But in John 14:1–6, Jesus warned them not to remain in a worried state of mind. He was telling us all: Don't succumb to a troubled heart. Don't give in to panic. Don't cave in to anxious care. We aren't to let our hearts remain in a state of agitation, panic, terror, or of being upset.

I may not be able to avoid being frightened on occasion. I may be unable to avoid flashes of panic or aches of anxiety. Perhaps I can't totally escape the temptation to worry. But I can avoid remaining in such a state or abiding in such a condition. In fact, it's my obligation as a Christian to fight off the sin of anxiety just as I would resist the sin of drunkenness, profanity, lust, or idolatry.

This passage is incredibly helpful in fighting the sin of worry (which is unbelief), and it also helps us in times of grief. I often use it at funerals, using this simple outline:

- The peace Jesus provides (John 14:1)
- The place Jesus prepares (John 14:2–4)
- The path Jesus prescribes (John 14:6)

Verse 3 is at the center of this text; and in memorizing it, notice how every phrase emphasizes a different aspect of our Lord's promised return. He is going away for the express purpose of preparing a place for us; He will return, and where He is, we will always be.

MEMORY TIP

In our list of 100 verses, we're including John 14:1, 2, 3, and 6. Why not go ahead and learn verses 4 and 5, too? It's one of the Bible's most reassuring paragraphs.

※ The belief of Christ's second coming, of which He has given us the assurance, is an excellent preservative against trouble of heart. —Matthew Henry

24. John 14:6

Jesus told him, "I am the way, the truth, and the life. No one comes to the Father except through Me."

On board the missionary ship *Duff* one Sunday in December 1796, Captain James Wilson told his passengers, "I was the youngest of nineteen children. While I was still a lad, my father, a ship captain, took me to sea. I grew up amid influences of the worst kind. When the war with the American colonies broke out, I enlisted in the king's service and fought in the bloody battle of Bunker Hill. Returning to England, I secured a berth on one of the vessels of the East India Company."

While sailing toward India, Wilson said, his ship was captured, and he was thrown in jail. One night, learning he was to be sold into slavery, he jumped from the prison ramparts into an alligator-infested river. Wilson escaped the river only to be captured. He was stripped, bound, and marched five hundred miles. "How I survived that terrible march or the tortures of prison, I cannot explain," he said.

At length, however, he was returned to England where, at age thirty-four, he met Pastor John Griffin. "In three hours of conversation, Griffin convinced me of the weakness of my belief in natural religion and planted in my mind certain truths which led to my conversion. The text he used with convincing effect was John 14:6."

Wilson purchased a ship and became the first to transport missionaries to the South Pacific. In his preaching he repeatedly proclaimed John 14:6. It was also a verse he used to bolster his missionaries, saying: "Dwell much on John 14:6. Jesus is the only source of life abundant for discouraged Christians and the only source of eternal life and hope for a degraded race."

This is a timeless verse to learn. We should dwell much on it.

Compare John 14:6 with Acts 4:12, which says, "Nor is there salvation in any other, for there is no other name under heaven given among men by which we must be saved" (NKJV). Jesus is the only highway leading us to God; He is truth personified; He is the source and giver of eternal life—the only way of salvation. Thomas à Kempis said, "Without the way, there is no going; without the truth, there is no knowing; without the life, there is no living."

MEMORY TIP

Jesus' discourse on "Let not your heart be troubled" was interrupted by Thomas, who asked in John 14:5, "Lord, we don't know where You're going. How can we know the way?" Try imagining the tone of voice Thomas used. Was it gentle and sincere or edgy and argumentative? As you picture and replay the scene in your mind, you'll soon find you've memorized the entire passage—John 14:1–6.

※ Jesus is not one of many ways to approach God, nor is He the best of several ways. He is the only way.—A. W. Tozer

25. John 14:27

Peace I leave with you. My peace I give to you. I do not give to you as the world gives. Your heart must not be troubled or fearful.

This is one of the Bible's greatest verses about inner peace, spoken by our Lord in His upper room discourse (John 13–17) on the night He was betrayed. As the disciples listened to Jesus speaking that night, they must have cringed at the second and third words of the verse: *I leave.* Throughout the upper room discourse, Jesus sought to prepare His disciples for His death, resurrection, and departure from earth. But as He went to the cross, to the grave, and into the skies, He was planning to leave one aspect of Himself behind: *Peace I leave with you.*

And it wasn't just generic or generalized peace. It was His own internal realms of infinite peace: *My peace I give to you.* He wasn't bestowing it to them in a temporary, inconsistent, or conditional way: *I do not give to you as the world gives.* He was giving them a legacy of peace that had the power forever to banish fear and trouble from their hearts: *Your heart must not be troubled or fearful.*

Notice that this verse falls naturally into four phrases. You can memorize it one small sentence at a time. Realize that Jesus was speaking these words to you and me just as clearly and immediately as they were spoken to the disciples two thousand years ago. Once you memorize this verse, you can close your eyes and listen to Jesus saying it to you at any time.

Peace I leave with you. My peace I give to you. I do not give to you as the world gives. Your heart must not be troubled or fearful.

Norma Patterson of Portland, Oregon, called me the other day and told me about her aged parents. When they were in their nineties—her father was ninety-three—she came by to take them shopping. Her dad was in apparent good health for his age and had recently bought a tiller to use in his garden. The couple had their devotions together each morning and on this particular morning, the old gentleman had pulled a card from the Promise Box that said: "Peace I leave with you; my peace I give you. I do not give to you as the world gives. Do not let your hearts be troubled and do not be afraid" (John 14:27 NIV). They shared that with Norma, and then the old fellow went over to the easy chair to sit and wait for the shopping trip. He dozed off. When they tried to awaken him a few minutes later, he was in heaven. "How thankful we were," Norma told me, "for that final Scripture verse that served as the closing benediction to my father's earthly life."[48]

✳ So precious indeed is peace that it was the one legacy left us by our departing Lord.[49]—A. B. Simpson

26. Isaiah 26:3

*You will keep in perfect peace the mind that is dependent
on You, for it is trusting in You.*

I like the old King James Version for Isaiah 26:3–4: Thou wilt keep
him in perfect peace, whose mind is stayed on thee: because he trustest
in thee. Trust ye in the LORD for ever: for in the LORD JEHOVAH is everlasting strength.

Isaiah 26 was written by Isaiah for the land of Judah as a song of
praise for the blessings of the Messiah's kingdom (see v. 1). Among those
blessings is *perfect peace*. Verses 3 and 4 go together beautifully and provide one of the most meaningful and memorable passages in the Old
Testament. Notice how the verses proceed through these phrases and
phases:

1. **Perfect Peace.** The original Hebrew says that God will keep
    in *shâlom, shâlom* those whose minds are stayed on Him.
    The word *shâlom* means more than a cessation of conflict.
    It conveys the idea of wholeness, quietness of spirit, safety,
    blessing, happiness of heart. The double use of the word
    multiplies its intensity.

2. **Stayed Minds.** When we fix our thoughts on Jehovah, all
    other concerns shrink to the proper perspective. Colossians
    3:2 says, "Set your minds on what is above, not on what is
    on the earth." Romans 8:6 talks about the mind-set of the
    Spirit, which is life and peace. We must manhandle anxious
    thoughts, turning them forcibly toward Christ and making our
    minds "stay" on Him.

3. **Abiding Trust.** In doing so, we trust Him more and more.
    Faith is the Bible's great antidote to fear, and faith grows
    stronger as we focus it on Christ instead of on crises. We
    acknowledge the difficulty but keep our focus on the Deliverer.

4. **Everlasting Strength.** As we stay our minds on Him, trust
    Him, and experience His perfect peace, we find daily strength

for daily needs. We have strength sufficient, strength eternally. *Thou wilt keep him in perfect peace, whose mind is stayed on thee: because he trusteth in thee. Trust ye in the LORD for ever: for in the LORD JEHOVAH is everlasting strength.*

Favorite Passage of the Hymnists

- Augustus Toplady was spurred to write the hymn, "Rock of Ages," from the marginal note in verse 4, which calls God our "Rock of Ages."
- The hymn, "Like a River Glorious," says, "Stayed upon Jehovah, hearts are fully blest, / finding as He promised, perfect peace and rest."
- Edward Bickersteth published a hymn that said: "Peace, perfect peace, in this dark world of sin? / The blood of Jesus whispers peace within."
- Another beloved hymn adds, "O this full and perfect peace! / O this transport all divine! / In a love which cannot cease, / I am His and He is mine."

※ Perfect, yet it floweth fuller ever day; perfect, yet it growing deeper all the way.—Frances Ridley Havergal

27. Isaiah 53:5

*But He was pierced because of our transgressions, crushed
because of our iniquities; punishment for our peace was
on Him, and we are healed by His wounds.*

The cross is at the crossroads of every book, chapter, and verse in the
Bible, and we clearly see that emphasis in Isaiah 53. This is a miraculous
portion of Scripture, giving us an advance look of the life, death, and resurrection of our Lord. Though written hundreds of years before Christ,
it's chockablock with prophetic details about the passion of the Messiah.
The images are so Calvary-vivid that it's amazing to realize it was written
hundreds of years before Jesus was born.

But Isaiah 53 doesn't just give us the details of Christ's history in
advance; it explains the purpose of it. *We* are the reason He was *pierced*
and *crushed* and *punished* and *wounded.* His gruesome death was redemptive in nature. The underlying theme is found by noticing several phrases
in this verse: *because of our transgressions . . . because of our iniquities . . .
our peace . . . we are healed.*

The cross wasn't a mere accident of history or a random act of vio-
lence. As the next verse puts it: "We all went astray like sheep; we all
have turned to our own way; and the Lord has punished Him for the
iniquity of us all."

So as you study Isaiah 53:5, adopt it as a personal verse. It's not only
prophetic; it's purposeful. The great emphasis reverberating through
every verse is redemption. Why was Jesus born? Why did He come from
the root and stock of David? Why did He grow up an ordinary-looking
man? Why did He suffer rejection, arrest, scourging, and crucifixion? *He
was pierced because of our transgressions, crushed because of our iniquities.*

Isaiah has been called the "Fifth Gospel" because it's packed
with Messianic prophecy. In Isaiah we keep running into
direct, detailed information about Jesus. The most poignant
passage is Isaiah 53. While memorizing verses 5 and 6, take
time to read this chapter carefully. Notice the incredible series
of predictive details about the Messiah and His death, which
can be arranged chronologically under these headings:

- Introduction: An opening summary of the Messiah (52:12–15)
- His birth and early years (53:1–2a; compare with 11:1)
- His appearance (v. 2b)
- His rejection by men (v. 3)
- His being forsaken by God (v. 4)
- His scourging and piercing (v. 5)
- His silence before His accusers (v. 7)
- His imprisonment and death (v. 8)
- His burial (v. 9)
- His resurrection (v. 10a)
- His postresurrection work (vv. 10b–11)
- His exaltation and glory (v. 12)

※ This chapter is so replenished with the unsearchable riches of Christ
that it may be called rather the Gospel of the evangelist Isaiah than the
prophecy of the prophet Isaiah.—Matthew Henry

28. Isaiah 53:6

We all went astray like sheep; we all have turned to our own way; and the LORD has punished Him for the iniquity of us all.

Solomon Ginsburg was born in Poland in 1867 to a Jewish rabbi who named him after the most glorious of the kings of Israel. Rabbi Ginsburg envisioned his son becoming a spiritual leader for Eastern European Jews. One night when Solomon was thirteen, he and his father were celebrating the Feast of Tabernacles in a small tent near their home. Solomon picked up a book of Hebrew prophets and turned randomly to Isaiah 53, which he read. His curiosity was stirred. "To whom does the prophet refer in this chapter?" he asked his father. His question was greeted with silence, so he repeated it. This time his father slapped him across the face.

Years passed. Solomon moved to London and took a job in a dry goods store owned by his uncle, an orthodox Jew.

"One Sabbath afternoon while passing through Whitechapel Street," Ginsburg recalled, "I met a missionary to the Jews—a converted Jew— who invited me to hear him preach at the Mildmay Mission to the Jews on the 53rd chapter of Isaiah. Now, I was particularly interested in this certain chapter of the Bible because . . . I could not but remember that scene in the tent and, of course, went, out of curiosity, to see if he had a better explanation to give than the one my father had given.

"That was the turning point. I went to hear him explain that marvelous prophetical chapter and though I could not understand it all at that time, it sank into my heart. He asked me to read the New Testament, and when he called my attention to the wonders of the life of the Messiah and how every prophecy was fulfilled in Jesus, I was soon convinced that the Son of Mary, the crucified One, was the Christ of God, the Messiah of Israel, the Rejected One of my people."[50]

Ginsburg was abandoned by his family, beaten and nearly killed by angry friends; but he became a powerful evangelist and missionary with enough adventures to fill an autobiography and whose lifelong message was the Messiah of Isaiah 53:6.

This verse begins with *we all* and ends with *us all*. It follows verse 5 naturally, and the two verses should be memorized side by side. Both are at the heart of the Old Testament's greatest chapter on the atoning death of the coming Messiah. The details of Christ's crucifixion as given predictively in Isaiah 53, coupled with its personal and universal application, have convinced multitudes of people to follow Jesus Christ. In the stories of Jewish converts to the Lord Jesus, this passage is frequently mentioned.

※ As trait after trait swings into focus and fulfillment, can we write any other name under Isaiah's amazing portrait of the sublime Sufferer in chapter 53 than Jesus of Nazareth?[51]—J. Sidlow Baxter

P R A I S E :

Worship and Thanksgiving

29. 1 Peter 1:3

> *Blessed be the God and Father of our Lord Jesus Christ.*
> *According to His great mercy, He has given us a new*
> *birth into a living hope through the resurrection of*
> *Jesus Christ from the dead.*

If you were a sentence, what mark of punctuation would follow you?

Is your life a question mark because you're without answers? A comma because you're in transition? A period for everything's at a standstill? Or a dash because you're in a continual rush?

This verse can put an exclamation point to our lives. It's a verse of praise; it begins with *Blessed be. . . .* It's a verse of worship, centered around *the God and Father of our Lord Jesus Christ.* It's a verse of joy, for *He has given us new birth into a living hope.* It's a verse of victory based on *the resurrection of Jesus Christ from the dead.* It's easy to memorize because it unfolds by itself and automatically divides into five great exclamations.

1. **Praise God!** In the Greek, Peter began with "Blessed be" and didn't come up for air until the end of verse 12. It's one long sentence. English translations chop this passage into a dozen

or so sentences; but in the original you get a sense of Peter's nonstop exuberance.

2. **Great mercy!** The reason for his excitement is God's great mercy. Peter had a lot of "oops" in his past. He could have kept on beating himself up, but he knew all his sins had been washed away by a flood tide of mercy.

3. **New birth!** That leads to the third exclamation: *He has given us a new birth.* Jesus Himself used this analogy when He spoke to a Jewish leader in John 3, telling him, "You must be born again."

4. **Living hope!** The new birth leads to living hope. Peter wasn't just speaking of an uplifting intangible. In the next verse he describes "an inheritance that is imperishable, uncorrupted, and unfading, kept in heaven for you." We have a yearning for eternal life in a real place with meaningful activity and worshipful living. Heaven! That's what mercy provides.

5. **Risen Savior!** It's *through the resurrection of Jesus Christ from the dead.* When Jesus died, He assumed the guilt that belongs to us. When He rose, He defeated sin, death, hell, and the grave.

No wonder Peter began his book with the praise word, *Blessed!* He saw the risen Christ, and it instantly changed his gloom to joy. When he later wanted to write the letter of 1 Peter, he began with the excitement of Easter. Peter wrote this letter approximately three decades after Christ's resurrection, yet his excitement was unabated. He still felt the exuberance he'd experienced years before as though it had happened yesterday. For Peter every day was Easter.

※ The resurrection is the pivot on which all of Christianity turns. . . . Without the resurrection, Christianity would be so much wishful thinking, taking its place alongside all other human philosophy and religious speculation.[52]—John MacArthur

30. Psalm 100:4

Enter His gates with thanksgiving and His courts with
praise. Give thanks to Him and praise His name.

Psalm 100 is one of the shortest and most exuberant passages in the
Bible. It takes about thirty seconds to read; and if you'll read it aloud
every morning for a month, you'll automatically have all five verses
memorized for the rest of your life. There are no negatives in this passage, no sorrows, warnings, or problems. It's just shouting and singing
and knowing and being thankful.

Notice the imagery of verse 4. The psalmist is writing against the
backdrop of the temple worship of the Old Testament. He's telling
the people of His day to come to Jerusalem, to the temple. Enter its gates
with a thankful spirit and come into the temple courts with praise.

Most of us don't live in Jerusalem, and the Jewish temple is no longer standing; but we can do exactly as the writer says whenever we pray,
whenever we praise God in private, and whenever we attend corporate
worship services at church or elsewhere.

Enter His gates with thanksgiving and His courts with praise. Give
thanks to Him and praise His name.

One Sunday night in 1742, evangelist John Wesley ventured
into a downtrodden section of Newcastle-on-Tyne, in the
north of England. He was appalled at the physical and moral
squalor. Joined by an associate, Wesley stood on the corner
and sang the 100th Psalm. Before long a crowd gathered,
and John began preaching. Soon more than a thousand
people were listening; and it was the beginning of a great
work, which made Newcastle a powerhouse for Methodism
in the English north.

�֎ All people that on earth do dwell,
Sing to the Lord with cheerful voice.
Him serve with fear, His praise forth tell;
Come ye before Him and rejoice.

The Lord, ye know, is God indeed;
Without our aid He did us make;
We are His flock, He doth us feed,
And for His sheep He doth us take.

O enter then His gates with praise;
Approach with joy His courts unto;
Praise, laud, and bless His Name always,
For it is seemly so to do.

For why? The Lord our God is good;
His mercy is forever sure;
His truth at all times firmly stood,
And shall from age to age endure.
—William Kethe, 1561

31. Psalm 100:5

For the LORD is good, and His love is eternal; His faithfulness endures through all generations.

A preacher of olden days, Rev. W. Durban of Chester, England, once preached a sermon of three points from this verse. He talked about: (1) the Inexhaustible Fount—the Lord's goodness; (2) the Ever-flowing Stream—His eternal love; and (3) the Fathomless Ocean—His ever-enduring faithfulness.

I can't beat that, but I would like to suggest a simple outline for the entire psalm that may aid you in memorizing it. Psalm 100 falls into two stanzas, and both begin with a call to worship. Verses 1–3 tell us to praise God with *gladatude.* We're to shout joyfully. Verses 4–5 tell us to praise Him with *gratitude,* to enter His gates with thanksgiving.

Gladatude and *gratitude* are appropriate for every situation in life. Several years ago Martin and Gracia Burnham were serving with New Tribes Mission when they were kidnapped by terrorists. During their year in captivity, they faced near starvation and were sometimes caught in the middle of gun battles. In the end both were shot. Martin was killed, but Gracia lived to tell the story. She said that near the end of their ordeal, one of the passages of Scripture that sustained them was Psalm 100. One night Martin said, "You know, Gracia, I don't know why the Lord has allowed this to happen, but today I've been thinking about Psalm 100, how we can serve the Lord with gladness. Just because we're here doesn't mean we can't serve Him with gladness, so let's serve the Lord with gladness." That night Martin was shot and killed, and Gracia was wounded in the firefight. But those words from Psalm 100 never died in her heart. "The Lord has given me joy," was her testimony.[53]

Matthew Henry's Outline

The great commentator Matthew Henry summarized this psalm by listing its seven reasons for entering His gates with thanksgiving.

1. The Lord is God, the only living and true God, infinitely perfect, self-existent, incomprehensible.

2. He is our Creator, for it is He that has made us, and not we ourselves.

3. He is therefore our rightful Owner, and we are His. To Him we belong.

4. He is our sovereign Ruler. We are His people, His subjects.

5. He is our bountiful Benefactor. We are not only His sheep but the sheep of His pasture, the flock of His feeding. He gives us all good things richly to enjoy.

6. He is a God of infinite mercy and goodness, a fountain that can never be drawn dry.

7. He is a God of inviolable truth and faithfulness. His truth endures to all generations, and no word of His shall ever be revoked or become antiquated.

※ It is with good reason that many sing this psalm very frequently in their religious assemblies . . . and if our hearts go along with the words, we shall make melody in it to the Lord.—Matthew Henry

32. Revelation 4:11

Our Lord and God, You are worthy to receive glory and
honor and power, because You have created all things,
and because of Your will they exist and were created.

According to my friend Frank Fortunato, director of music for OM International, Revelation 4–5 is the favorite passage for many worship leaders. It's arguably the Bible's primary text on the subject of worship, a virtual open window into an actual worship service occurring in heaven. As you memorize Revelation 4:11, think of the verse as a summary of the whole scene around the throne; but take time to study the entire two-chapter passage. Here's an outline to help.

1. **When we worship, we're approaching a glorious throne (Rev. 4:1–3).** In the heart of heaven is a literal throne; and this throne is the ultimate power source for the universe. It's described many times in the Bible (for example, Isa. 6 and Ezek. 1), and whenever we worship, we're approaching this throne of grace and glory.

2. **When we worship, we're joining an eternal chorus (Rev. 4:4–11).** Worship is constantly occurring around the throne. The twenty-four elders may be symbolic of the universal church, and the four living creatures may represent the angelic world. I don't think our life in heaven is literally going to be one long church service; we'll be involved in many things throughout eternity. But whenever we want, we'll be able to walk up the broad boulevard in New Jerusalem, heading toward the city center; and as we approach the throne, we'll hear the music and feel the ground vibrating under our feet. We'll join a song in sweet accord and thus surround the throne.

3. **When we worship, we're praising a triune God (Rev. 5:1–10).** Notice the Trinity in these chapters. In chapter 4 God the Father is emphasized. Revelation 5 is a description

of God the Son. In both chapters we have a reference to the Holy Spirit (Rev. 4:5 and 5:6; compare with Rev. 1:4).

4. **When we worship, we're glorifying a worthy Lord (Rev. 5:11–14).** He is worthy to receive glory, honor, and praise.

Worship is the gyroscope of the soul. A person without personal patterns of worship is like a ship or an airplane without any stabilization or direction. When we worship, we are aligning our minds to God's truth, our imaginations to God's glory, our emotions to God's stability, and our souls to God's songs. When we worship, we are approaching a glorious throne, joining an eternal chorus, praising a triune God, and glorifying a worthy Lord, saying: "You are worthy, O Lord, to receive glory and honor and power; for You created all things, and by Your will they exist and were created" (Rev. 4:11 NKJV).

※ In Revelation 4 and 5 . . . all the host of heaven joins the angels, elders, a heavenly choir, and ten thousand times ten thousand in singing and playing songs to the Lord.[54]—Vernon Whaley

PROMISES:

Verses to Stand On

33. Matthew 6:33

> *But seek first the kingdom of God and His righteousness,*
> *and all these things will be provided for you.*

After ditching their plane in the Pacific during World War II, Captain Eddie Rickenbacker and his crew were adrift twenty-four days. Their ultimate survival was due, in large part, to a waterproof New Testament; and one of their most cherished passages was Matthew 6:31–34. "That's the best thing I've heard yet," said one of the men, listening to this passage. "Read it again, Colonel."[55]

Matthew 6:19–34 is our Lord's definitive teaching about the sin of worry. Once you memorize its core verse, Matthew 6:33, you'll be leaning on it again and again, too. Here's an outline of the passage as it unfolds. Study it as you work on this great verse.

1. **Worry indicates a defective value system (Matt. 6:19–25).** There are more important issues than food, clothing, houses, and entertainment.
2. **Worry indicates a defective self-image (Matt. 6:26).** We're more valuable than anything else God has made, including the birds of the air.

3. **Worry indicates a defective way of thinking (Matt. 6:27).**
   Anxiety doesn't add one hour to our lives or one cubit to our
   height. It's a useless exercise and an inefficient way of thinking.
4. **Worry indicates a defective trust in God (Matt. 6:28–30).**
   Faith is the ability to maintain inner strength by trusting in
   the promises of God amid the problems of life. We shouldn't
   fall into the "you of little faith" camp.
5. **Worry indicates a defective purpose in life (Matt. 6:31–33).**
   If we take care of things that are important to God, He'll take
   care of things that are important to us.
6. **Anxiety indicates a defective view of tomorrow
   (Matt. 6:34).** In this verse Jesus specifically tells us to deal
   with today's issues and don't worry about tomorrow's.

Rosalind Goforth, veteran missionary to China, wrote an
uplifting little book entitled *How I Know God Answers Prayer*,
in which she first tells of practicing this verse as a child.
Easter Sunday came one year during a warm springtime,
and everyone had put away their winter clothes. Rosalind
had no Easter dress, and she decided she'd rather stay home
than wear her winter garb. Going to her room, she opened
her Bible, and her eyes rested on Matthew 6:33. "It was as if
God spoke the words directly to me," she said. Why worry
about your clothes? Seek first His kingdom. She put on her
old dress and fought off a feeling of humiliation as she went
to church. The Easter message touched her deeply; and the
next day a box arrived from a distant aunt, containing not
only new dresses but many other things as well.[56]

※ Seek ye first the Lord, and then He will provide for you everything
that is profitable for you in this life and He will crown it with everything
that is glorious in the life to come.[57]—Charles Spurgeon

34. Romans 8:28

*We know that all things work together for the good of
those who love God: those who are called according to
His purpose.*

Romans 8:28 is the favorite verse of millions around the world.
It's arguably the greatest promise in the Bible, for it summarizes all the
others. It's the biblical basis for optimism and the promise that morphs us
into resilient sanguines, whatever our temperament. It's God's darkroom
in which negatives become positive. It's His situation-reversal machine
in which heartaches are changed into hallelujahs. It is the foundation of
hope and a fountainhead of confidence. Even our failures can become
enriching, and our sins can be redeemed. Even death itself becomes a
blessing for the child of God.

Romans 8:28 is all inclusive, all powerful, and always available. It is
as omnipotent as the God who signed and sealed it. It's as loving as the
Savior who died to unleash it. It can do anything God can do. It can
touch any hurt and redeem any problem. It isn't a mere platitude but a
divine promise. It isn't a goal but a guarantee. It isn't wishful thinking
but a shaft of almighty providence that lands squarely on our pathway
each day and every moment.

The Lord moves heaven and earth to keep this promise. He puts His
eye to the microscope of providential oversight and scans the smallest
details of our lives, working them into a tapestry of blessing, making sure
goodness and mercy follow us all our days.

In memorizing this verse, remember that the first part is the promise;
the last half is the condition. The first part tells us what God will do in
working all things for our good. The last part gives us our responsibil-
ity—to love Him and be true to His purposes in our lives. Memorize
Romans 8:28, and you need never despair again![58]

Everything that happens to you is for your own good. If the waves roll against you, it only speeds your ship toward the port. If lightning and thunder come, the rain clears the atmosphere and promotes your soul's health. You gain by loss, you grow healthy in sickness, you live by dying, and you are made rich in losses.

Could you ask for a better promise? It is better that all things should work for my good than all things should be as I would wish to have them. All things might work for my pleasure and yet might all work my ruin. If all things do not always please me, they will always benefit me.

This is the best promise of this life.[59]—Charles H. Spurgeon, on Romans 8:28

※ We cannot fully understand now, but when we stand upon the heights of glory, we shall look back with joy on the things we have suffered, for we shall know then that our severest trials were a part of the "all things" which worked together for eternal good.[60]—John A. Broadus

35. Jeremiah 29:11

"For I know the plans I have for you"—this is the LORD's declaration—"plans for your welfare, not for disaster, to give you a future and a hope."

Here's a verse you often see on wall plaques. It's sometimes inscribed in beautiful calligraphy or printed over soaring pictures of eagles. It's found on coffee mugs and decorative plates. But few people have studied its context.

Jeremiah 29 is a letter Jeremiah sent to displaced Jewish captives who'd been dragged from their homes and resettled in refugee camps in Babylon. Other prophets were claiming God would perform a miracle and deliver the nation of Judah as He'd done in the past. Jeremiah's message was the opposite, saying in effect: "The Lord will not save us this time. Our sins have so alienated us from Him that only judgment is left. And yet even the judgment of God is merciful. It may take seventy years, but God will reestablish our nation, and His ultimate plans are undeterred. His purposes are stubborn things and will win in the end." It's in this context we find verse 11.

Here's a simple study guide for the passage, which will aid in understanding and memorizing the key verse. After giving the background in verses 1–3, Jeremiah advises the exiles:

1. **Make the best of things (vv. 4–6).** Settle down, decide you're in for the long haul, go on with life, and make the best of it. Build houses. Plant gardens. Get married. Have children. Be hopeful. Don't give up. You may not be where you want to be, but make the most of where you are. Don't spend your years wishing that something had or hadn't happened. Don't be consumed by things you cannot change. Just settle down and do the best you possibly can where you are.

2. **Pray where you are (v. 7).** Pray for the nation in which you're exiled. Pray for the *shalom* of the country where you're located. Lift up your surrounding circumstances by prayer.

3. **Beware the wrong voices (vv. 8–9).** Don't listen to false hope or ungodly messages.

4. **Take the long view (v. 10).** At this point Jeremiah gives his famous prophecy that after seventy years God would bring the captives of Judah back and restore the nation of Israel. Our long-term prospects are always better than our immediate conditions.

5. **Get hopeful about God's plans (v. 11).** This is our key text, our memory verse.

6. **Seek the Lord above all (vv. 13–14).** The next couple of verses remind us that since God has plans to prosper us and to give us hope and a future, we must seek Him with all our hearts.

✳ Verse 11 is a powerful promise to claim when you are "in exile." God thinks about you personally and is planning for you. . . . You need not fear the future.[61]—Warren Wiersbe

36. 1 John 1:7

But if we walk in the light as He Himself is in the light,
we have fellowship with one another, and the blood of
Jesus His Son cleanses us from all sin.

Years ago evangelist Charles Finney preached this verse in Detroit, and afterward a stranger asked him to come to his house to talk with him about his soul. Against the advice of friends, Finney followed the man down a side street, into an alley, and through a darkened door into the back of an establishment. The man reached into his pocket and pulled out a revolver. He said, "You see this revolver? It has killed four people. . . . Is there any hope for a man like me?"

Finney simply repeated the text from his sermon: "The blood of Jesus Christ cleanses us from all sin."

The man explained he owned a saloon and had sold every kind of substance to every kind of person. Again he asked, "Is there any hope for a man like me?"

And again Finney replied, "The blood of Jesus Christ cleanses us from all sin."

The man continued, "In back of this other partition is a gambling joint and . . . there isn't a decent wheel in the whole place. . . . Men have gone out of that gambling place to commit suicide. . . . Is there any hope for a man like me?"

Finney said, "The blood of Jesus Christ cleanses us from all sin."

The man confessed he had cheated on his wife and been abusive to his family. Hanging his head, he asked, "Brother Finney, is there any hope for a man like me?"

Finney took the man by the shoulders and said, "Oh, son, what a black story you have to tell! But God says, 'The blood of Jesus His Son cleanses us from all sin.'"

The next night this man and his family came to Finney's meeting, listened to the gospel, and gave themselves to the Lord Jesus Christ.

The blood of Jesus His Son cleanses us from all sin.

Charles Finney used this verse evangelistically, but in its actual context it's addressed to Christians. John was writing to church members, encouraging them to walk in the light and to confess their sins in order to keep their relationship with the Lord sweet and strong. We need to walk in the light.

Perhaps there's a sin into which you repeatedly fall. It's unhealthy to allow that sin to remain unconfessed. If we know Jesus as our Savior, we don't lose our salvation every time we sin, but we do lose something of the sweetness we should have with our heavenly Father. We lose a clear conscience and an untarnished walk. How wonderful to confess our sins and walk in the light as He is in the light.

※ I find a speedy deliverance by simply declaring over and over again "The blood of Jesus cleanseth me from all sin." It seems as if Satan cannot endure the mention of that name; he always takes his flight. —Hannah Whitall Smith

37. 1 John 1:9

*If we confess our sins, He is faithful and righteous
to forgive us our sins and to cleanse us from all
unrighteousness.*

One Sunday as I was preaching in my church in Nashville, I said that
Christians need to keep "short accounts" with God. We need to confess
our sins quickly and completely so that no corrosion builds up on our
spiritual connections with God. I was interrupted by a young man whom
I'd never seen before and have never seen since. Jumping to his feet, he
shouted, "Sir! Sir! That's not right."

He had the salutary effect of waking up everyone instantly. "When
we receive Christ as Savior," he insisted, "He forgives our sins past, present, and future. We never again need to confess sins that are forgiven in
His sight."

It's true that all our sins are instantly and forever forgiven—past,
present, and future. Yet Jesus taught us to pray, "Forgive us our debts,
as we also have forgiven our debtors" (Matt. 6:12). And, as I reminded
my young heckler that evening, 1 John 1:9 was expressly written to
Christians. According to the next paragraph, 1 John 2:1–2, John wrote
his book to retard sin in our lives ("I am writing you these things so that
you may not sin"), but he added, "If anyone does sin, we have an advocate
with the Father—Jesus Christ the righteous One."

It's not that we're saved and lost, lost and saved, over and over. It's a
matter of maintaining constant, conscious fellowship with our Lord. It's
obviously possible for Christians to sin. I've never met one who didn't.
That doesn't mean we've lost our salvation; but sin does jeopardize the
victory and vitality of our faith. Confession means we acknowledge our
failures and humbly ask God's help in overcoming them.

Some sins are so stubbornly addictive that it takes massive amounts of time, effort, confession, counseling, and rededication to conquer them. If you're struggling with a besetting sin, don't give up. Keep memorizing Scriptures related to your weakness. Keep anticipating its onset and avoiding its traps. Like Daniel, determine in your heart you aren't going to be defiled, and ask God for full and total victory.

We may never be perfect in this life, but through the power of the blood of Jesus Christ, we can have consistent victory over known sin; and 1 John 1:9 is a powerful verse to store in the armory of your mind.

※ We must confess our sins immediately. The reason the laver was polished so finely was to reflect the image of the person standing in front it, the person who came to wash his hands and feet. This is a picture of examining ourselves with the help of the Holy Spirit and confessing any sin we find. The Bible tells us, "If we confess our sins to Him, He is faithful and just to forgive us and to cleanse us from every wrong."[62] —Bill Bright

38. Proverbs 3:5

Trust in the LORD with all your heart, and do not rely on your own understanding.

If God can guide the birds in their migrations and the planets in their orbits, He has an appointed way for our lives and can lead us accordingly. Many biblical texts reassure us of divine guidance, and among the best is Proverbs 3:5–6. Taken together, we have three commands and one all-embracing promise.

THREE COMMANDS

1. **Trust in the Lord with all your heart.** We can lean on the Lord's promise because we can lean on the Lord Himself who is unchanging, unfailing, unerring, and illimitable.
2. **Do not rely on your own understanding.** This doesn't mean we shouldn't think through decisions or use our God-given minds. It means we think through things in total submission with God's will and in complete awareness of His superior knowledge about the things that concern us.
3. **Think about Him in all your ways.** Acknowledge Him by saying, "Lord, I want to turn this dilemma or decision over to You. I desire Your perfect will."

ONE PROMISE

1. **He will guide you in the right paths.** He will direct you in all your ways, giving you the wisdom to do what's best and providentially arranging the circumstances of life according to His will. He'll lead you in the right path.

Burleigh Law served as a jungle pilot in central Africa. One day he took off in clear skies, but shortly he noticed thunderclouds in the distance; and these thunderheads rushed together at startling speed. Burleigh frantically searched for an airstrip, but there was nowhere to land. Openings appeared in the clouds here and there, and he kept turning his plane toward them, following little patches of blue. It was like a needle threading its way through fabric. Burleigh was lost in the skies, depending entirely on visible navigation. Finally, spotting a little landing strip, he made it safely to the ground.

Suddenly a vehicle raced up to his plane, and a nurse jumped out and ran to the plane, shouting, "I don't know where you came from, but I know you are an answer to our prayers." This woman was staying with a missionary couple who had been isolated on a remote station for months. The unsettled political situation had left them cut off from outside communication. The roads were impassible and the bridges out. The missionary wife had become ill with fever and possible rabies. That morning they had called together the Christians in the village, and the church had earnestly prayed for God's guidance. That day, the Lord arranged the storm clouds to direct and guide Burleigh Law and his little plane to that spot of earth.[63]

He can direct our paths, even if they're in the clouds!

❋ Every morning, he walked into the Oval Office; he quoted Proverbs 3:5–6. That's how he started his day.[64]—Billy Zeoli about President Gerald Ford

39. Proverbs 3:6

*Think about Him in all your ways, and He will guide
you on the right paths.*

In the Sermon on the Mount, Jesus told us to enter the narrow gate,
for the gate is wide, and the highway is broad that leads to destruction,
and many are traveling that way. "How narrow is the gate and difficult
the road that leads to life" (Matt. 7:4), He said, "and few find it." When
memorizing Proverbs 3:6, we must prayerfully keep to the right path at
every point. Look over these other verses that contain the same three
words we see at the ending of Proverbs 3:6.

- Those who follow **the right path** fear the LORD.
  (Prov. 14:2 NLT)
- He will guide you on **the right paths**. (Prov. 3:6)
- I have taught you in the way of wisdom; I have led you **in
  right paths**. (Prov. 4:11 NKJV)
- Whoever abandons **the right path** will be severely
  disciplined; whoever hates correction will die.
  (Prov. 15:10 NLT)
- By forsaking **the right path** they have gone astray.
  (2 Pet. 2:15 The NET Bible)
- A sensible person stays on **the right path**. (Prov. 15:21 NLT)
- Those who put others on **the right path** of life will glow like
  stars forever. (Dan. 12:3 *The Message*)
- If another believer is overcome by some sin, you who are
  godly should gently and humbly help that person back onto
  the right path. (Gal. 6:1 NLT)
- Direct your children onto **the right path**, and when they are
  older, they will not leave it. (Prov. 22:6 NLT)
- Teach them to follow **the right path**. (1 Kings 8:36 NLT)
- Listen, my son, and be wise, and keep your heart on **the
  right path**. (Prov. 23:19 NIV)

- Keep on **the right path**, so the weak will not stumble but rather be strengthened. (Heb. 12:12 NCV)
- Teach me how to live, O LORD. Lead me along **the right path**. (Ps. 27:11 NLT)
- Show me **the right path**, O LORD; point out the road for me to follow. (Ps. 25:4 NLT)
- Lead me in **the right path**, O LORD . . . . Make your way plain for me to follow. (Ps. 5:8 NLT)
- He leads me along **the right paths** for His name's sake. (Ps. 23:3)
- He led them by **the right path** . . . . Let them give thanks to the LORD for His faithful love. (Ps. 107:7–8)
- Discretion will watch over you . . . rescuing you . . . from those who abandon **the right paths**. (Prov. 2:11–13)
- I praised the LORD, the God of my master Abraham, who had led me on **the right path**. (Gen. 24:48 The NET Bible)

※ Lord Jesus, when I begin to grow dizzy and faint because of what I see before me, draw my perspective back to You. Thank You, dear Shepherd, that You lead me in right paths.[65]—Hannah Hurnard

40. 1 Corinthians 10:13

> *No temptation has overtaken you except what is common to humanity. God is faithful and He will not allow you to be tempted beyond what you are able, but with the temptation He will also provide a way of escape, so that you are able to bear it.*

As I poured over this passage, I was surprised to discover that while it's a great verse for every Christian in the world, it's particularly addressed to veteran Christians who have been on the road awhile. At the end of the previous chapter, Paul admitted, "I discipline my body and bring it under strict control, so that after preaching to others, I myself should not be disqualified."

In chapter 10 he brought up the subject of the Israelites, who, having started toward the promised land with soaring aspirations, messed up en route. They passed through the Red Sea, feasted on manna, and drank water from the rock. But they were detoured by their own failings and faithlessness.

"Now these things . . . were written as a warning to us, on whom the ends of the ages have come," said Paul. "Therefore, whoever thinks he stands must be careful not to fall! No temptation has overtaken you except what is common" (1 Cor. 10:11–13).

Paul, a veteran missionary, struggled to remain disciplined in his life. The Israelites, having experienced the most unique set of miracles in the Old Testament, stumbled. However mature our Christian experience, we're not beyond the danger of those temptations common to everyone. But God is faithful. He will not allow us to be tempted beyond what we're able to bear but will provide a way of escape.

The Greek term for "a way of escape" was the word used for a passageway out of a canyon. Sometimes people wandered into ravines and couldn't see any pathway out. They thought they were trapped. But if they looked hard enough, there was a goat path somewhere, a way out.

Our best escape route is intentionally staying close to Christ on a daily and hourly basis. Having successfully resisted temptation Himself, He knows the way out of the canyon.

When athletes are arrested during brawls at places like strip clubs and dog fights, we say, "How stupid! Why would they risk their millions of fans and million-dollar contracts by deliberately putting themselves in the wrong place at the wrong time?" Yet we do the same thing when we go anywhere that exposes our hearts to needless temptation. It could be an entertainment venue, a girlfriend's apartment, a computer screen, a nightspot, some sort of catalog, or even a shopping mall. It's like the man who told his doctor that he had broken his arm in two places. The doctor said, "Well, stop going to those two places."

※ Temptation is the tempter looking through the keyhole into the room where you're living; sin is your drawing back the bolt and making it possible for him to enter.[66]—J. Wilbur Chapman

41. Psalm 55:22

Cast your burden on the LORD, and He will support you;
He will never allow the righteous to be shaken.

John Fletcher is known in history as the godly vicar of Madeley; but in 1755 he grew deeply discouraged. On Thursday, January 23, he felt so despondent he almost gave up hope. "Having continued my supplication till near one in the morning," he told his diary, "I then opened my Bible, and fell on these words, 'Cast thy burden on the Lord, and he shall sustain thee. He will never suffer the righteous to be moved.' Filled with joy, I fell again on my knees to beg of God that I might always cast my burden upon Him. . . . My hope was now greatly increased."[67]

This verse has often done the same for me. I recall learning it during my sophomore year in college, while despondent. My roommate, seeing my low spirits, showed me this verse, and it immediately struck a chord in my heart. I memorized it and have loved it ever since.

In Psalm 55 King David was distressed. A handful of people were causing him problems. We don't know if this is strictly personal (since David was, after all, a human with all kinds of emotions) or if it involved national security (since he was also head of state). In either case he had a handful of enemies, and one of them, a close friend and ally, had betrayed him and gone to the other side. David was devastated, and that's what occasioned this psalm (see vv. 1–3 and 12–14).

Whether it was personal, political, or both, David knew that a wound this deep had to be given over immediately and irretrievably to the Lord (see vv. 16–18). Regaining strength, he ended Psalm 55 with this exhortation to us: "Cast your burden on the Lord, and He will support you."

An ancient Jewish rabbi was carrying a heavy load on his back when he joined an Arabian tradesman with his caravan. Looking at the rabbi, the Arab said, "Take your burden and throw it on my camel." The rabbi later used that incident to illustrate this verse. When we cast our care on

the Lord, we're taking off our load and throwing our problems and worries onto His back.

This verse was the inspiration for a great German hymn
by Georg Neumark, one that should be known by every
Christian in the world: "If Thou but Suffer God to Guide
Thee," or, as the newer hymnals put it: "If You Will Only Let
God Guide You."

> *If thou but suffer God to guide thee, and hope in God
> through all thy ways, He'll give thee strength, whate'er
> betide thee, and bear thee through the evil days. Who
> trusts in God's unchanging love builds on the rock that
> naught can move.*[68]

※ God hears the call of those in need, the souls that trust in Him
indeed.—Georg Neumark

42. 1 Peter 5:7

*Casting all your care upon Him, because He cares about
you.*

This is the New Testament version of Psalm 55:22, and it's easy to
memorize if we absorb one word or phrase at a time.

- **Cast**. This word means "to throw, to remove something
  from one place to another." Where is your concern right
  now? Where is your worry? When you cast it on Him, you're
  removing it from your own heart and tossing it onto His.
  The Greek word used here only occurs one other time in
  the New Testament, in the story of the triumphal entry.
  Our Lord's disciples took their cloaks and *threw them on* the
  donkey as a saddle for the Lord Jesus.
- **All**. I'll never forget the night when, deeply worried, I saw
  this word "all." It struck me like an anvil. There are no
  exemptions, exceptions, or exclusions.
- **Your**. This is personal, for you. It means the unique set of
  circumstances that is troubling you at this moment.
- **Cares**. The Greek word means "worries and anxieties." This
  doesn't mean we shouldn't have healthy concern about things
  or give them prayerful thought. This is talking about the
  unhealthy, crippling, dysfunctional anxiety that can tear us
  down like a building being demolished.
- **On Him**. "Him" is God. We're to humble ourselves before
  Him, saying, "Lord, I have a problem I can't handle, but You
  can. I'm leaning on Your grace" (see vv. 5–6).
- **Because He cares about you**: This is the declaration on
  which the command is given. The command is that we cast
  our cares on Him. The basis of it is this; God really does care
  for us.

How Do We CAST?

- **C = Commit** yourself and your situation into the Lord's hands. He is our all in all. He is all sufficient for all needs and in all circumstances. All our burdens were nailed to His cross, and all our cares disappeared into the mouth of His vacant tomb.
- **A = Ask** God for His wisdom, strength, and guidance. Learn to make things a matter of prayer instead of a bird's nest of anxious care.
- **S = Surrender** your situation to God's will. Give Him permission to resolve it whenever and however seems best to Him, according to His wisdom.
- **T = Trust** Him. Begin acting as if all these things were going to work together for good. Adopt an attitude of hope and rest in the assurance that He reigns.

❋ Commit whatever grieves thee into the gracious hands of Him Who never leaves thee, Who Heav'n and earth commands. Who points the clouds their courses, Whom winds and waves obey, He will direct thy footsteps and find for thee a way.—Paul Gerhardt

Holiness:

Obeying God's Commands

43. 2 Chronicles 7:14

> *[If] My people who are called by My name humble*
> *themselves, pray and seek My face, and turn from their*
> *evil ways, then I will hear from heaven, forgive their sin,*
> *and heal their land.*

In the Bible the definitive book about revival is 2 Chronicles, and this is the key verse. It's addressed to those called by God's name, and it presents a 4/3 formula for revival.

THE REQUIREMENTS FOR REVIVAL

1. **Humble yourselves.** Pride is a beaver's dam that holds back the currents of personal and corporate revival.
2. **Pray.** History's great revivals have been prayed down by burdened souls.
3. **Seek His face.** Get serious about your relationship with Christ and the spiritual habits that draw us closer to Him.
4. **Turn from our wicked ways.** If we're doing anything careless, immoral, or disobedient, we must confess it and reestablish obedience to that area of life.

THE PROMISES OF REVIVAL

1. **I will hear from heaven.** God will listen to our prayers as carefully as He listened to Solomon's in 2 Chronicles 6.
2. **I will forgive their sin.** God specializes in forgiveness. There's not a sin on earth He'll not instantly and permanently forgive when sincerely confessed and placed under the blood of the cross.
3. **I will heal their land.** Has any land needed healing more urgently than ours? Has any generation needed revival more than this one?

As a young man, George Müller was spiraling downward, in and out of prison. A friend invited him to a Bible study, and that proved to be the turning point. Müller went on to establish missionary enterprises and mercy ministries, all of them operated by faith and prayer. When he published an account of his answers to prayer, copies made it to Ireland.

In January 1857 James McQuilkin, moved by Müller's book, started a prayer group of his own. Within two years, a spirit of revival broke out in a nearby church as McQuilkin preached. Excited Christians carried the fire to other places, and a revival blazed through Ireland. It's estimated that as many as a thousand people a day gave themselves to Christ. Business came to a standstill as people could do nothing else until they got right with God. Men were unable to sleep at night; they were under such conviction they wept and prayed through the night in their homes. Churches were packed at all hours. Divisions and conflicts evaporated. The jails were emptied. The churches were filled. The people became concerned for the poor, and the nation became almost like a new land. It's known today as the Irish Revival of 1859.[69]

✳ God at His own initiative voluntarily gave us, His people, the covenant of revival in 2 Chronicles 7:14. He must be true to His covenant word, and He wants for us to fulfill our part.[70]—Wesley Duewel

44. Romans 12:1

*Therefore, brothers, by the mercies of God, I urge you to
present your bodies as a living sacrifice, holy and pleasing
to God; this is your spiritual worship.*

Romans is the most important book in the Bible in setting forth
essential Christian theology. The first eleven chapters explain the doctrine of justification by grace through faith. The last five chapters begin
here in chapter 12 with the word *therefore.* They tell us how to live as
those who have been justified by God's mercy.

Our foremost obligation is to offer our bodies as living sacrifices,
holy and God pleasing. This is the essence of spiritual worship. In the
Old Testament, sacrifices were slain, but New Testament Christians are
to be *living* sacrifices. When we consider this, it makes sense of the work
we do, the fatigue we feel, the burdens we bear, and the sacrifices we
make for Christ's kingdom.

In 1930 Arthur and Ethel Tylee, with their infant daughter Marian,
lived in a remote spot of Brazil, seeking to reach the Nhambiquara tribe
with the gospel. One autumn day the Nhambiquara attacked the station.
Arthur and Marian were among those slain. Ethel, though injured, stag-
gered six kilometers for help.

In her anguish Ethel longed to have been among those who died. She
didn't know how she could possibly go on. But then, as she later wrote,
"Romans 12:1 came to my mind: 'I beseech you . . . by the mercies of
God, that you present your bodies a living sacrifice, holy, acceptable to
God.' I thought, 'It will be harder to be a living sacrifice than a dying
sacrifice, but I must be.'"

Armed with that verse, Ethel Tylee devoted the rest of her life to traveling across the United States as a living sacrifice, speaking in churches,
conferences, and colleges, presenting the challenge of reaching lost tribes
for Jesus.[71]

Ethel's verse is equally applicable to you and me. Today and every
day, let's offer our bodies as a living sacrifice for Him.

When Corrie ten Boom was eighty years old, she spoke from Romans 12:1 in Copenhagen, urging her audience to be living sacrifices. Afterward, two young nurses invited her to their apartment for lunch, and she went with them—only to discover they lived on the tenth floor, and there was no elevator.

Corrie struggled up the stairs one step at a time, complaining to herself the whole way. Finally reaching the apartment, she met the parents of one of the girls. Sharing the gospel with them, she had the joy of leading them to Christ. On her way down Corrie said, "Thank you, Lord, for making me walk up all these steps. And next time, Lord, help Corrie ten Boom listen to her own sermon."[72]

❋ If you are a Christian, your life is not your own. Rather than dying, however, God asks you to live for Him as a living sacrifice. Every day, you are to offer your life to Him for His service.[73]—Henry T. Blackaby

45. Romans 12:2

Do not be conformed to this age, but be transformed by
the renewing of your mind, so that you may discern what
is the good, pleasing, and perfect will of God.

Dr. Martin Luther King once told of riding the bus across town every day to attend high school. In those days blacks were required to sit at the backs of buses while whites sat in the front. Even if there weren't any white people on the bus, blacks still could not sit in the front. If all the "black seats" were occupied, riders had to stand over the empty seats reserved for whites. "I would end up having to go to the back of that bus with my body," said Dr. King, "but every time I got on that bus I left my mind up on the front seat. And I said to myself, 'One of these days, I'm going to put my body up there where my mind is.'"[74]

Dr. King was stating an essential, inviolable rule in life. Our bodies usually end up where our minds are. Our brains are a complex aspect of God's creation, and our minds are the fountainhead of our lives. "For as he thinketh in his heart, so is he" (Prov. 23:7 KJV). Marcus Aurelius wrote, "The most important things in life are the thoughts you choose to think." Ralph Waldo Emerson added, "A man is what he thinks about all day long."

Every temptation comes to us via our thoughts, making the mind the battleground of the soul.

When we come to Christ, a change begins in our minds and thinking. We—our personalities and everything about us—are transformed by the renewing of our thoughts. The Greek word for "transformed" is *metemorpho* from which we get our word *metamorphosis*. We experience an inner metamorphosis as our minds are renewed by God's Spirit and His Word. The *Phillips Version* puts it like this: "Don't let the world around you squeeze you into its own mold, but let God remold your minds from within, so that you may prove in practice that the plan of God for you is good, meets all his demands, and moves toward the goal of true maturity."

Key Bible Texts about the Mind

- Test me, LORD . . . examine my heart and *mind*. (Ps. 26:2)
- Give me an undivided *mind* to fear Your name. (Ps. 86:11)
- You will keep in perfect peace the *mind* that is dependent on You. (Isa. 26:3)
- Set your *minds* on what is above, not on what is on the earth. (Col. 3:2)
- You are being renewed in the spirit of your *minds*. (Eph. 4:23)
- Love the Lord your God . . . with all your *mind*. (Matt. 22:37)

❉ [Transformation] happens by the renewing of our minds, and the way our minds become renewed is by the study of the life-giving and renewing Word of God.[75]—James Montgomery Boice

46. Romans 12:11

Do not lack diligence; be fervent in spirit; serve the Lord.

This is one of the biggest little verses in the Bible, for it gives us a three-pronged injunction about doing the Lord's work each day. We need an attitude of diligence, fervor, and servanthood. The word *diligence* comes from a Greek term having to do with speed. It means "hastily, eagerly, promptly, with earnestness and zeal." I love the way it's put in the New International Version: *Never be lacking in zeal, but keep your spiritual fervor, serving the Lord.*

Perhaps the best thing ever written about Christian zeal comes from the pen of the inimitable Bishop J. C. Ryle of Liverpool. In 1852 he published a tract entitled "Be Zealous," saying that zeal is a subject no reader of the Bible can pass over:

> *Zeal in religion is a burning desire to please God, to do*
> *His will, and to advance His glory in the world in every*
> *possible way. It is a desire which the Spirit puts in the*
> *heart of every believer when he is converted—but which*
> *some believers feel so much more strongly than others,*
> *that they alone deserve to be called zealous. It impels*
> *them to make any sacrifice, to go through any trouble,*
> *to deny themselves to any amount, to suffer, to work, to*
> *labor, to toil, to spend themselves and be spent, and even*
> *to die, if only He can please God and honor Christ.*
>
> *They see only one thing, care for one thing, live for one*
> *thing, are swallowed up on one thing, and that one thing*
> *is to please God. Whether they live or whether they die;*
> *whether they have health or sickness, whether rich or*
> *poor; whether they please others or give offense; whether*
> *they are thought wise or foolish; whether they get blame*
> *or praise; whether they get honor or shame—for all this*

the zealous person cares nothing at all. He burns for one thing; and that one thing is to please God and to advance God's glory.

"I want to strike a blow at the lazy, easy, sleepy Christianity of these latter days, which can see no beauty in zeal, and only uses the word 'zealot' as a word of reproach. I want to remind Christians that 'Zealot' was a name given by our Lord to His Apostle Simon as a mark of honor, and to persuade them to be zealous men. . . . There is in a sense in which it may be said that zeal is contagious. Nothing is more useful to the adherents of Christianity than to see a real live Christian—a thoroughly zealous man of God."
—J. C. Ryle

❋ Zeal is good for a Christian's own soul. . . . It will help mightily to promote inward feelings of joy, peace, comfort, and happiness. None have so much enjoyment of Christ as those who are ever zealous for His glory.[76]—J. C. Ryle

47. Romans 12:12

Rejoice in hope; be patient in affliction; be persistent in prayer.

On June 22, 1879, the great Victorian preacher, Charles Spurgeon, preached a sermon on this text in which he said the first two phrases—*rejoice in hope* and *be patient in affliction*—are powerful antidotes against poison, but they must be taken with prayer. "Joy and patience are curative essences," he said, "but they must be dropped into a glass full of supplication, and then they will be wonderfully efficient."

These are the Great Physician's three prescriptions for tough times: *Rejoice in hope; be patient in affliction; be persistent in prayer.* Take each phrase in turn, memorize it, meditate on it, consider its implications, then go on to the next.

Rejoice in hope. When we can't rejoice in circumstances, we can rejoice in the anticipation of what God's going to do with them, in them, through them, despite them, and because of them. On cloudy days the sun still shines as brightly as ever in the center of the solar system; and when we rejoice in hope, we're saying, "Despite current conditions, the Son is shining for me as brightly as ever with healing in His rays."

Be patient in affliction. Rejoicing in hope enables us to be patient in affliction. *Patience* is *hope* in different clothing. It's the ability to wait calmly as the Lord works everything in conformity with the purpose of His will.

Be persistent in prayer. "Whenever your hope seems to fail you and your joy begins to sink," said Spurgeon, "the shortest method is to take to your knees. By remembering the promise in prayer, hope will be sustained and then joy is sure to spring from it." An open Bible and a bowed head create a powerful atmosphere in which God's will is brought to bear upon the distresses of life. Jesus even recommended we "nag" God with our requests, like a persistent neighbor at a friend's door or a relentless widow harassing a presiding judge.

Romans 12:12 is a shot in the arm for whatever ails us.

Rejoicing In . . .

- *Rejoice in* all the good things the LORD your God has given you. (Deut. 26:11)
- *Rejoice in* the presence of the LORD Your God. (Deut. 27:7)
- *Rejoice in* the shadow of [His] wings. (Ps. 63:7)
- *Rejoice in* . . . praise. (Ps. 106:47)
- *Rejoice in* the way revealed by [His] decrees. (Ps. 119:14)
- *Rejoice in* the Holy One of Israel. (Isa. 29:19)
- *Rejoice in* [His] house of prayer. (Isa. 56:7)
- *Rejoice in* the hope of the glory of God. (Rom. 5:2)
- *Rejoice in* hope. (Rom. 12:12)
- *Rejoice in* the Lord always. (Phil. 4:4)

※ Prayer brings us into that state of grace where tribulation is not only endured, but where there is under it a spirit of rejoicing.[77] —E. M. Bounds

48. Romans 12:18

If possible, on your part, live at peace with everyone.

In 1757 Benjamin Franklin sailed for England aboard a ship that joined a fleet of nearly one hundred others. From the deck Franklin noticed that the water behind most of the ships was churning and agitated; but two ships had calm wakes, as though gliding through the sea. Asking the captain about it, he received this reply: "Oh, everyone knows that. The cooks on those two ships have just thrown their greasy water overboard."

Franklin spent years pondering this phenomenon. He even designed a walking cane with a hollow center that he filled with oil. When at a lake or river, he'd amaze his friends with a little parlor trick. No matter how choppy the water, when he poured his oil onto the surface, it became more calm. The calmness would spread out and cover a wide area.

Franklin's discovery was the object of much inquiry. People wanted to know why a thin layer of oil could create such calm on the waters. The answer is simple. Ripples and waves are caused by the friction between air and water. When a gust of wind blows over a body of water, the air grabs at the water and lifts it up. When the surface of the water is coated with oil, the friction is reduced, and the wind cannot easily get hold of the water.

What oil is to water, grace and graciousness are to our relationships. People tend to rub one another the wrong way. The friction between our personalities creates ripples of disharmony. But when we pour the oil of grace onto the water, it has a way of calming the seas. If we're gracious to people—we don't get mad easily; we don't stay mad long; we don't take offense or let a root of bitterness spring up—if we forgive easily and assume the best in others, and if we learn to smile through the day, we'll have a much happier life. So will the people around us!

In ten words Romans 12:18 sums up the essence of good relationships. The main clause is found in the last five words: *live at peace with everyone.* But it opens with two helpful caveats: (1) if possible, and (2) on your part. That tells us that sometimes, despite our best efforts, we'll have broken friendships, rocky relationships, and even hostile enemies. Even the author of these words, the apostle Paul, had a falling out with Barnabas, a disagreement with Peter, and a conflict with Alexander the Coppersmith, among others. But the list of his friendships in Romans 16 shows us that he surely kept his own advice: *If possible, on your part, live at peace with everyone.*

MEMORY TIP

To remember the reference, think of 12:18 as the opposite of 1812. When we think of 1812, we think of war; when we think of 1218, we think of living at peace.

❈ A fool's displeasure is known at once, but whoever ignores an insult is sensible. . . . A person's insight gives him patience, and his virtue is to overlook an offense.—King Solomon, Proverbs 12:16; 19:11

49. 2 Corinthians 9:7

Each person should do as he has decided in his heart—
not out of regret or out of necessity, for God loves a cheer-
ful giver.

Since money is all-pervasive in our lives, it seems only right to
devote at least one of our memory verses to the subject of giving. The
greatest stewardship chapters in the Bible are 2 Corinthians 8 and 9. In
2 Corinthians 9:7, these two chapters are reduced to their key principles:

1. **Each one should give faithfully.** The New King James
   Version says: "So let each one give." We can take the words
   "each one" literally. Every Christian. I believe even children
   should tithe. Childhood is when we learn healthy patterns of
   living; and what's healthier than giving? An allowance is the
   first opportunity in a person's life to discover the blessings of
   giving. If every child in every Christian home learned that the
   first dime of every dollar belonged to the Lord, God's work on
   earth would never be underfunded.

2. **Each one should give thoughtfully,** as he has decided in
   his heart. It's all right to give impulsively; but Christian
   stewardship involves planned, consistent, thoughtful patterns
   of giving. J. L. Kraft, who founded Kraft Foods, said, "The
   only investments I ever made which have paid constantly
   increasing dividends is the money I have given to the Lord."

3. **Each one should give freely,** not out of regret or necessity. We
   don't give because we're compelled to; we're excited about the
   privilege and blessings of it.

4. **Give cheerfully.** This verse tells us God loves cheerful givers,
   which is a remarkable phrase. I can't think of another time
   in the Bible when a similar phrase occurs. We see lots of
   references to God's love, but I can't recall another attitude or
   activity in life that's commended in this way. The Bible seems
   to be saying that *God is excited about us when we are excited*

about giving. And that leads to the wonderful promise in the next verse: *And God is able to make every grace overflow to you, so that in every way, always have everything you need, you may excel in every good work.*

In the book *Tortured for Christ,* Richard Wurmbrand tells of being in and out of Communist prisons because of his faith in Christ. The principle of tithing was so internalized in his heart and those of his fellow prisoners that when they received a slice of bread a week and dirty soup every day, they faithfully tithed from it. Every tenth day they gave their soup to weaker brothers, and every tenth week they took their slice of bread and gave it to fellow prisoners in Jesus' name.[78]

※ Earn all you can, save all you can, and then give all you can. Never try to save out of God's cause; such money will canker the rest. Giving to God is no loss; it is putting your substance into the best bank.[79] —Charles H. Spurgeon

50. Hebrews 10:25

*Not staying away from our meetings, as some habitually
do, but encouraging each other, and all the more as you
see the day drawing near.*

Hebrews 10:25 is the best church-going verse in the Bible, warning us against missing worship services. Indeed, our attendance should
increase as the Lord's return draws nearer. Why?

1. **Because of the rhythm of life God established.** In Genesis,
   God rested on the seventh day of creation. It wasn't that He
   was tired. He paused to enjoy what He'd done the previous six
   days and to transition to the next period of time. He was also
   establishing a pattern of one day in seven for rest and worship,
   which was later embodied in the Ten Commandments.
   When Jesus rose from the dead on the first day of the week,
   Christians began observing Sunday as their Sabbath, and the
   pattern was the same—one day in seven for rest and worship.
   It is built into the rhythm of the universe and into the pace
   and pulse of our bodies and souls.

2. **Because of the pattern of worship Scripture prescribes.**
   Luke 4:16 says of Jesus, "As usual, He entered the synagogue
   on the Sabbath day." Most scholars believe synagogues
   developed during the Babylonian Captivity so the Jews could
   gather weekly for worship wherever they were. Three things
   happened in those meetings: praise, prayer, and precept. The
   early church, made up almost entirely of Jewish people, met
   for the same purpose—praise, prayer, and the instruction of
   Scripture.

3. **Because of the family of God Christ has created.** Ephesians
   1:5 (NLT) says: "God decided in advance to adopt us into his
   own family by bringing us to himself through Jesus Christ.
   This is what he wanted to do, and it gave him great pleasure."
   There's no such thing as a solitary saint. Christianity is about

relationships. The phrase "one another" occurs about fifty times in the New Testament.

4. **Because of the work of God to which we're called.** The local church is the only institution Jesus established on earth. He didn't found hospitals, civic clubs, mission agencies, Bible colleges, or crisis centers. Many of these other organizations come out of the local church and are sponsored by it. But the local church is Ground Zero for God's work on this earth. The church is God's agenda for this world.

We need a weekly countercultural experience to counter the culture we're in. We must counteract the popular culture in our lives. When we go to church, we're participating in a global weekly network of people doing the same thing at the same time; we're participating in an ancient practice that goes back to the origins of the church and to the very beginning of the creation and involves all God's people of every epoch and age; and we're involved in a habit that the Bible says is increasingly vital as time draws to a close.

✳ There is something wrong with our Christianity when we have to beg most of our crowd to come to church to hear about it.[80] —Vance Havner

51. Proverbs 1:7

The fear of the LORD is the beginning of knowledge; fools despise wisdom and instruction.

In memorizing 100 key texts of the Bible, notice that four of them come from the book of Proverbs (Prov. 3:5–6; 1:7; 15:1). We could just as easily have selected all 100 verses from this book because it's the most practical, everyday, commonsense book in Scripture.

Think of the book of Proverbs as God's Twitter feed to the human race. With Twitter, you have 140 characters for your message or to sum up what's going on in your life. These little messages are short bursts of communication. When you read a tweet—a Twitter message—you're reading a burst of truth about a person's life, activities, observations, or philosophy, summed up in 140 characters or less.

That's just what we have in the book of Proverbs: God's giving advice to us in short bursts of communication, usually 140 characters or less per verse.

Proverbs is God's divinely designed self-improvement course, His textbook for learning how to wise up and live. The 915 verses in Proverbs represent God's wisdom for the hundreds of situations we step into each day.

Think of Proverbs as portable wisdom—heavenly rules for earthly living.

God's wisdom has little to do with grades on a report card but everything with getting high marks in life. It isn't just data accumulation or brainpower. It is putting our knowledge to work in everyday life. Thumb through the thirty-one chapters of Proverbs, and you'll find them packed with advice about working hard, eating wisely, watching how much we drink, guarding how much we speak, avoiding unhealthy friendships and immoral sexuality, treating people kindly, handling money well, and making good decisions in matters great and small.

The whole theme of Proverbs is summed up in today's memory verse, Proverbs 1:7. This verse is the key that unlocks the whole book, and that's why it's worth memorizing. There is one common denominator to all the Proverbs, a single thread that runs through each verse: *The fear of the Lord is the beginning of knowledge; fools despise wisdom and instruction.*

Each of the Proverbs either tells us: (1) how we will respond to life if we have a healthy fear of the Lord, or (2) how we will mess up if we don't.

The fear of the Lord is not unhealthy, dysfunctional, or debilitating fear. It means an appropriate respect, reverence, awe, and wonder. A. W. Tozer wrote: "The fear of God is . . . astonished reverence. I believe that the reverential fear of God mixed with love and fascination and astonishment and admiration and devotion is the most enjoyable state and the most satisfying emotion the human soul can know."[81]

The fear of the Lord is the beginning of knowledge; fools despise wisdom and instruction.

※ It is one of life's strange turns that scholars ransack libraries looking for wisdom, while, perhaps, the janitor has found it long ago.[82]
—Vance Havner

52. Proverbs 15:1

*A gentle answer turns away anger, but a harsh word stirs
up wrath.*

The book of Proverbs is packed with verses about our tempers and
our tongues. If you need some help with anger management or mouth
control, read through Proverbs with a red pencil, circle every verse you
find on these topics, then type them on your computer or write them
on a page in your notebook. Read over your list, find the best verse for
you, and memorize it. After you have memorized it, learn the second best
verse for you; and so on until the power of God's Word melts away the
hardened habits of tongue and temper.

You might want to start with Proverbs 15:1. This verse applies particularly to the *tone* of our voices. It talks about a gentle answer or a harsh
word. The adjectives *gentle* and *harsh* have more to do with the way we
speak than what we actually say. Many times we speak the right words
with the wrong attitude, making a good situation bad or a bad situation
worse. Other verses in Proverbs govern the *contents* of what we say, but
Proverbs 15:1 is devoted to the intonation, inflection, volume, pitch, and
timbre of our voices. It includes the expression on our face and the body
language behind our words.

Want to be wise, mature, less stressed, and less stressful to others?
Become a Proverbs 15:1 person.

Professor Robert Webber relays a childhood memory of living near a cantankerous farmer. One day Robert strayed over the property line and picked a bucket of blackberries on the neighbor's land. The man burst out the front door, waving his fists and shouting threats. Robert ran home and told his dad what had happened, and the two marched over to the neighbor's house. Robert thought his dad would tell the old farmer a thing or two. But when the man came to the door, Mr. Webber said, "Mr. Farmer, I'm sorry my son was on your property. Here, I want you to have these blackberries."

The man was disarmed. "Hey," he said, "I'm sorry I yelled at the boy. . . . I don't even like blackberries. You keep them. And you can pick all the berries you want."

Walking back home, Mr. Webber looked down at his son and said, "The Scripture says, 'A soft answer turns away wrath.' Remember that, Robert."

Years later Robert Webber wrote, "I've not always lived up to that Scripture, or to the example of my father, but I've never forgotten those words or my dad's action that gave those words meaning."[83]

※ Grievous words stir up anger as certainly as an effect follows its cause. . . . For the moment they seem to be smart and spirited, betraying a dignified temper and a haughty courage, but in reality, they are nothing more than proofs of littleness, spitefulness, chagrin, or other emotion lying on the same degraded line.[84]—Joseph Parker

FULLNESS:

The Holy Spirit's Role in Our Lives

53. Ephesians 5:18

And don't get drunk with wine, which leads to reckless actions, but be filled with the Spirit.

Have you ever been accused of LUI? A drunk driver may be charged with DUI, which means "driving under the influence." But when people with the Holy Spirit in their bloodstream are spotted, there should be evidence of *living under the influence.* That's the simplest way I know to explain the contrast and comparison in this verse between being drunk and being Spirit filled.

In Ephesians 5:18, we have a clear contrast (don't do *this*, but do *this*); but it's a contrast based on comparison. The apostle Paul could have told us not to lose our temper but to be filled with the Spirit. He could have said, "Don't hate your neighbor, but be filled with the Spirit."

Yet the contrast is between being drunk and being Spirit filled.

This is the third time the New Testament mentions this parallel. We read in Luke 1:15 that John the Baptist "will be great in the sight of the Lord and will never drink wine or beer. He will be filled with the Holy Spirit from his mother's womb." And on the day of Pentecost when the Holy Spirit burst upon the 120 believers in the upper room, people scoffed, "They're full of new wine!" But Peter responded, "These people are not drunk, as you suppose, since it's only nine in the morning. On the contrary, this is what was spoken through the prophet Joel: 'And it will be in the last days, says God, that I will pour out My Spirit'" (Acts 2:13–17).

When we are *living under the influence* of the Holy Spirit, we're controlled and empowered by Jesus Christ, and He has full access and influence in every corner and quadrant of our lives. Being Spirit filled is being Christ centered. It means that Jesus controls us and is living His life through us. It has an exuberance that could almost be compared with being under the influence of alcohol. *Don't get drunk with wine, which leads to reckless actions, but be filled with the Spirit.*

On a hot South Carolina evening in September 1981, I learned about being filled with the Spirit. Kneeling at an old sofa at the end of an upstairs dormitory hallway, I asked the Lord, as best I could, to take control of my life and fill me with Himself and with His Spirit. I felt no electrical charges; but when I went to bed that night, I could hardly sleep. I was tremendously excited about Jesus Christ, and I couldn't wait till the next morning to tell someone that I had given myself fully to Him. I've never gotten over the experience. I hope I never will.

※ Let us not forget that the Spirit within us is the presence of Christ. If we are filled with the Spirit, it is Christ Himself who fills us.[85]
—René Pache

54. Ephesians 5:19

*Speaking to one another in psalms, hymns, and spiritual
songs, singing and making music to the Lord in your
heart.*

Ephesians 5:18–20 is Paul's definitive treatment about being filled
with the Spirit, so it's helpful to memorize the whole (short) paragraph.
This is one of the most important passages in the Bible about the reality
of daily Christian living.

In the upper room discourses of John 13–17, Jesus explained that He
had to return to heaven but would send another Comforter who would be
with us and *in* us forever. After His resurrection Jesus ascended to heaven
as promised, and ten days later the Holy Spirit was poured out on the
early church, as described in Acts 2.

Now when we receive Christ, we're actually receiving the Holy Spirit
who applies the finished work of Christ to our lives. Through the Holy
Spirit, Jesus comes to live within us. As we live in yielded obedience and
faith, we're filled with His Spirit, living under His influence.

The first and most natural by-product is a song in our hearts. Notice
the unbroken nature of this passage: "Be filled with the Spirit, speaking
to one another in psalms, hymns, and spiritual songs, singing and making music to the Lord in your hearts."

We're to sing: (1) to one another, joining voices and encouraging
one other with songs of praise; and (2) to the Lord.

We're to do it: (1) with our voices in speaking and singing; and
(2) in our hearts.

We're to do it with psalms, hymns, and spiritual songs. Experts
debate the differences among the three terms, but it makes sense to think
of them in epoch terms. Psalms are hymns from biblical history. Hymns
are those from Christian history. Spiritual songs are expressions of worship that are more contemporary to our own generation. Ephesians 5:19
makes a case for what's often called "blended worship."

The primary point, however, is this: the first evidence of being filled with the Spirit is a singing heart.

Four times the New Testament tells us that, in some wonderful sense, the Holy Spirit represents the presence of Jesus Himself via the Spirit.

- When they came to Mysia, they tried to go into Bithynia, but the *Spirit of Jesus* did not allow them. (Acts 16:7)
- But if anyone does not have the *Spirit of Christ*, He does not belong to Him. (Rom. 8:9)
- I know this will lead to my deliverance through your prayers and help from the *Spirit of Jesus Christ*. (Phil. 1:19)
- They inquired into what time or what circumstances the *Spirit of Christ* within them was indicating when He testified in advance to the messianic sufferings and the glories that would follow. (1 Pet. 1:11)

✳ Singing I go along life's road, praising the Lord, praising the Lord. Singing I go along life's road, for Jesus has lifted my load.—Eliza E. Hewitt

55. Ephesians 5:20

Giving thanks always for everything to God the Father in the name of our Lord Jesus Christ.

When our girls were younger, I enjoyed reading to them every night at bedtime. One of the books we enjoyed was about a little boy named Alexander who struggled through a day in which everything seemed to go wrong for him. Shortly afterward I had a day that started the same way. Midway through the morning, I sat down for my devotions and spontaneously wrote a few lines in my journal: "I woke up late, and Grace was late to school today (again), and the trash cans had to be taken out, and the dog nuzzled his dirty nose against my white overcoat, and the drive-in window at McDonald's took five times longer than usual, and they poured my coffee out of an old pot, and I just know it's going to be a terrible, horrible, no good, very bad day."

I hadn't planned on writing those words; they just showed up on the paper. As I read them, I thought of Alexander and burst into laughter. And I had one of the best days I've had in a long time. It's all in our attitude.

Yesterday as I was flying back to Nashville from Tulsa, the weather forecaster in Oklahoma warned us that there would be terrible storms across the Southeast, so I was concerned about my flight. But the pilot pierced the clouds and got us above them. As I looked down on those magnificent, billowing, brilliant clouds, I thought to myself that storms are beautiful from the upper side.

We all have terrible, horrible, no good, very bad days. We all have stormy days. But when we're filled with the Spirit—when we've placed every part and parcel of our lives under the control of Jesus Christ—it affects our attitude. We fly at a higher altitude. We find ourselves always giving thanks to God the Father through our Lord Jesus Christ.

After all, if all things work together for good, as Romans 8:28 promises, why not always give thanks in all things?

Teaching Others about Being Filled with the Holy Spirit from
Ephesians 5:18–21

1. *A command.* Be filled with the Spirit.
2. *A contrast.* Don't be drunk with wine, but be filled with the
   Spirit.
3. *A comparison.* Being under the influence of the Spirit shares
   some surprising comparisons with being under the influence of
   alcohol (see Acts 2:1–15).
4. A change. How do we know if we're filled with the Spirit?
   Certain changes will occur in our lives: singing in our hearts
   (v. 19), gratitude in our minds (v. 20), and submission in our
   attitudes (v. 21).

※ A grateful mind is a great mind; a thinking person is a thankful
person.—Anonymous

56. Ephesians 5:21

Submitting to one another in the fear of Christ.

I miss the days when gas stations did the pumping. When I was learning to drive, gasoline was eighteen cents a gallon. As we pulled into the station, we'd run over a cable that rang a bell summoning an attendant. We'd say, "Fill 'er up," or, "Give me a dollar's worth." While the gas was pumping, someone would check our oil, clean the windshield, and check the tires.

So much for progress.

At least now some cars talk to us and tell us when we're low on fuel, how many miles we have left, and where the closest station is. But my car isn't so fancy. I still have to keep an eye on the gauge.

If there were a gauge on your forehead that indicated whether you were filled with the Holy Spirit or empty, what would it read? Where would the needle fall?

Ephesians 5:19–21 gives us three gauges: singing, thanksgiving, and submission. Each attitude bores more deeply into our personalities. It's relatively easy to burst into song, more difficult to be thankful on rough days, and harder still to remain humble in our relationships.

Furthermore, these attitudes transfer immediately into our marriages, which is the subject of the next paragraph (vv. 22–33). Going on into chapter 6, this attitude of submission is applied to the parent-child relationship (6:1–4), and even to the workplace (6:5–9).

If we are filled with the Holy Spirit, it shows on these three dials: singing, thanksgiving, and submission. This obviously isn't a one-time event, nor does it happen suddenly. It's a process, a habitual life of growing in the Spirit-filled, Christ-centered life.

Don't tell the Lord, "Give me a dollar's worth." Say every day, "Fill 'er up!"

True humility, the pith of godliness, doesn't mean developing an unhealthy self-image but a healthy image—not of ourselves—but of the Lord Jesus. It's thinking realistically of ourselves and optimistically of Him. It isn't thinking little of ourselves; it's thinking of ourselves less and less and of Him more and more.

Humility doesn't go around groveling in the dirt and saying, "I'm an idiot. I'm no good. I'm cheap. I'm worthless." After all, we're the climax and crown of His creative genius, made in His image. We're worth more than many sparrows; we're worth so much Christ died for us. We're heirs of God and joint heirs of Christ. Humility isn't a matter of saying, "I'm worthless!" It's saying, "He is worthy!"

If pride is the soil of sinfulness, humility is the heart of holiness. It's the basic bread-and-butter attitude of: "Jesus first, others second, and I'll take the leftovers. I'm sent to serve."

※ The humble man feels no jealousy or envy. He can praise God when others are preferred and blessed before Him. He can bear to hear others praised and himself forgotten.[86]—Andrew Murray

57. Galatians 5:22

But the fruit of the Spirit is love, joy, peace, patience, kindness, goodness, faith.

If a farmer taped artificial apples to the trees in his orchard, it might look good at a distance; but no one would be fooled for long. Genuine fruit is produced from within. We don't need artificial attitudes or synthetic personality traits. We need the genuine love, joy, peace, patience, kindness, goodness, faithfulness, gentleness, and self-control of Jesus Christ.

Galatians 5:16–26 is all about walking with Jesus Christ by means of the Holy Spirit. Verses 16, 18, and 25 tell us to live by the Spirit, to be led by the Spirit, and to keep in step with the Spirit. We can walk with Jesus just as surely as the two disciples did in Luke 24; but now it's via His ever-present Spirit. As we do this, there are two results:

1. **We minimize our faults (vv. 16–21).** When we live by the Spirit, we won't gratify the desires of the sinful nature, and we'll be increasingly able to overcome the lusts of the flesh, which are listed in this passage.

2. **We maximize our fruits (vv. 22–23).** When we live by the Spirit, we'll begin to develop nine attitudes that make up the Christian personality, and these are listed in verses 22–23 as the "fruit of the Spirit." These traits describe perfectly the personality of Jesus of Nazareth. It's a description of His character. If you had to make a list of nine words to describe Jesus, this would be the list. The only way to develop more love, joy, peace, and all the rest is to abide in Him.

When God created the world, He built the same patterns and principles into both the physical and spiritual realms. That's why we can illustrate spiritual truths with physical realities like trees and grapevines.

- Psalm 1 says that when we meditate on Scripture we're like fruit trees planted by rivers of water.
- The writer of Psalm 52 compared himself to an olive tree in the house of God.
- Psalm 92 likens us to trees that still bear fruit in old age and who stay fresh and green.
- Jeremiah 17 says that when we trust in the Lord we're like trees planted by the water, the leaves of which are always green even in drought times.
- The blind man who Jesus healed said at first that he saw people like trees walking.
- Jesus used a slightly different analogy when He said in John 15 that we're like branches connected to the grapevine of Himself.
- Galatians 5:22–23 compares us to grapevines that should be bearing fruit if the sap of the Holy Spirit is flowing unhindered through our branches.

※ Every time we say, "I believe in the Holy Spirit," we mean that we believe there is a living God able and willing to enter human personality and change it.[87]—J. B. Philips

58. Galatians 5:23

Gentleness, self-control. Against such things there is no law.

If we're rooted and grounded in Christ, the sap of the Holy Spirit takes the nutrients of the Word, disseminating it through our systems, and producing a life of fruitfulness. The word *fruit* means "attitudes." The evidence walking with Christ is a growing set of distinctive attitudes.

1. **Love.** This is the first on the list because it's the superlative attitude, the fountainhead of all the rest.

2. **Joy.** Love is something we convey to others, but joy is something that lights up our own lives. Joy lifts our own hearts. As that happens, of course, other people are the beneficiaries, including our family members and work associates. The word *joy* is found more than two hundred times in the Bible, and the corresponding word *rejoice* is found about two hundred more times.

3. **Peace.** This is the quality of calmness and inner strength keeping us steady during tough times. Peace is acting as though God had already worked out the solutions to all our problems, which is true for every child of God.

4. **Patience.** There are two kinds of patience. The first one is related to circumstances, and we call that perseverance. The second is related to people, and we call that being even tempered. These are qualities of the spiritual life that develop within us as we walk with Christ.

5. **Kindness.** This is the practical side of the first quality on the list—love. It's when our love expresses itself in countless ways, large and small (but usually small).

6. **Goodness.** The word *goodness* is used here in a moral sense. It means being morally sound. It's the practical side of holiness.

7. **Faith.** Many versions translate this word as *faithfulness*. We're trustworthy of character because we trust Him who is worthy.

8. **Gentleness**. The Bible frequently commands us to be strong of spirit yet warm and friendly in our dealings with others.

9. **Self-Control**. This comes at the end of the list because it's like the knot at the end of the string that keeps the pearls from slipping off the necklace and spilling onto the floor.

These nine qualities are listed as one "fruit" because they are compared to grapes on a cluster. As we abide in the vine of Jesus Christ, the Holy Spirit progressively matures this cluster of attitudes in our personalities. This is what distinguishes believers from everyone else on earth.

One of the challenging aspects of memorizing Galatians 5:22–23 is getting the nine "fruit" in the right order. Perhaps this prayer will help. It's built on the first letter of each of the virtues—LJPPKGFGS: *Lord Jesus, please produce kingdom grace for God's sake.*

❊ I am the vine; you are the branches. The one who remains in Me and I in him produces much fruit, because you can do nothing without Me.—Jesus, in John 15:5

JOY:

God's Kind of Happiness

59. Psalm 118:24

This is the day the LORD has made; let us rejoice and be glad in it.

God is in the day-making business. The Ancient of Days is the Manufacturer of Days. He has a continually running conveyer belt stretching from the sun to the earth and from heaven to this world. One new day rolls off God's assembly line every twenty-four hours, right on schedule, each one unique. We rise from bed each day knowing that an endless succession of sunrises and sunsets come from the workbench of His will, all of them individually crafted, packaged with grace, wrapped in love.

This verse reminds us that God's compassions never fail; they are new every morning, for great is His faithfulness. Goodness and mercy follow us all the days of our lives; and as our days may demand shall our strength ever be.

In its context Psalm 118:24 is Messianic. The author composed this psalm to be sung by the crowds approaching the temple during great worship festivals in Jerusalem; and this is the song the children sang as Jesus entered Jerusalem on Palm Sunday. He is the stone, rejected by the builders, who became the cornerstone (vv. 22–24).

In his book *Shadows on the Wall,* devotional writer F. W. Boreham told of preaching in a particular church during his college days. His lodgings were with Old Bessie, the elderly widow of the former pastor; and Boreham was given the room she normally occupied. He rose the next morning and threw open the blinds. There, etched in the glass, were the words, "THIS IS THE DAY." At breakfast he asked her about it.

"I had a lot of trouble in my time," she explained, "and I am a great one to worry. I was always afraid of what was going to happen tomorrow. And each morning when I woke up I felt as though I had the weight of the world upon me. Then one day, when I was very upset about things, I sat down and read my Bible. It happened that I was reading the 118th Psalm. When I came to the 24th verse, I stopped. *This is the day that the Lord hath made; we will rejoice and be glad in it....* It flashed upon me like a burst of sunshine on a gloomy day."

Snatching up a glass-cutting tool from the kitchen, Old Bessie ran upstairs and scrawled the words on the windowpane. "There!" she thought. "Now I shall see that little bit of Bible every morning when I draw up the blind, and I will say to myself, 'This is the day!'"[88]

MEMORY TIP

The verse reference is easy to remember. Each day is composed of twenty-four hours the Lord has made—Psalm 118:24.

※ This is the day the Lord hath made;
He calls the hours His own;
Let Heav'n rejoice, let earth be glad,
And praise surround the throne.—Isaac Watts

60. Philippians 4:4

Rejoice in the Lord always. I will say it again: Rejoice!

According to reports, anxiety is epidemic in the United States; more Americans suffer from anxiety (in proportion to population) than any other country on earth. Anxiety affects forty million Americans, and three of the top-ten drugs are for mental illness.

The Bible is a medicine chest of antidepressant verses and tranquilizing passages. Scripture is full of therapeutic theology, and this paragraph in Philippians 4 is my favorite anti-anxiety passage in the Bible, worth memorizing every word. Philippians 4:4–9 is Paul's personal six-point strategy for mental peace.

The first step is in verse 4: *Rejoice in the Lord always. I will say it again: Rejoice!* Perhaps you're thinking: *You can't just tell someone to be happy. You can't just command joy.* Why not? Why can't we choose our own attitudes? When we make ourselves smile, the very act of smiling lifts our spirits and makes it easier for us to pull out of discouragement.

But notice this is a qualified statement. It tells us to rejoice *in the Lord.*

We may not be able to rejoice in our load, but we can rejoice in our Lord. We may find no joy in our situation, but we can rejoice in our Savior. To rejoice in the Lord means we rejoice in our unassailable, unchanging relationship with the sovereign Lord and in His qualities, gifts, promises, and attributes.

Deuteronomy 26:11 says we should rejoice in all His gifts. We're to rejoice in His goodness in 2 Chronicles 6:41. Psalm 9:14 tells us to rejoice in His salvation. Psalm 31:7 says we should rejoice in His love. Psalm 89:16 says that we can rejoice in His name all day long. Psalm 119:14 tells us to rejoice in His statutes as in great riches. Psalm 119:162 tells us to rejoice in God's promises. Isaiah 65:18 commands us to rejoice in what God has created. We're to rejoice in the bounty of God in Jeremiah 31:12, and Romans 5:2 tells us to rejoice in the hope of the glory of God.

The first step to overcoming the stranglehold of worry is to determine to do as God says here: rejoice in the Lord always.

The Bible doesn't always give "six easy steps," but here in Philippians 4, we have a bullet-pointed list for experiencing inner peace.

- Rejoice in the Lord. (v. 4)
- Be gracious with others. (v. 5a)
- Remind yourself of God's nearness. (v. 5b)
- Cast out worry. (v. 6a)
- Pray with thanksgiving. (v. 6b)
- Focus your mind on what is excellent and praiseworthy. (vv. 8–9)

Two promises are connected with these principles: the peace of God will guard your heart and mind (v. 7), and the God of peace will be with you (v. 9).

※ The joy Christ gives is for time and eternity, for soul and body, for adversity and prosperity.[89]—William A. Swets

61. Philippians 4:5

Let your graciousness be known to everyone.
The Lord is near.

Here are the next two steps into a peaceful mind: be gracious to others and remind yourself of God's nearness.

Paul was writing to the church in the city of Philippi, one of the dearest congregations in the New Testament. They were generous to Paul, sending him financial help time and again. But there was internal strife in the church, and at the beginning of chapter 4, Paul addressed it: "I urge Euodia and I urge Syntyche to agree in the Lord."

Have you noticed that interpersonal relationships are a major source of stress? Most of the things we worry about involve other people in one way or another. Perhaps we're not getting along with coworkers or fellow church members; or perhaps there's tension in our home.

If we can't put out all the fires, at least we can lower the temperature by being gentle and gracious. That doesn't mean being weak or fragile. It means we're moderate in our reactions and pleasant in our demeanors. Let your graciousness be known to everyone.

The third step in overcoming worry is to remember the closeness of our Lord: "The Lord is near." There are two ways to interpret this, in terms of either time or space. Paul may have meant the Lord's return is near, making this a reference to the second coming. Or he might have meant the Lord's presence is near us all the time. Both are true, but it seems to me that the second is preferable.

We don't need to worry, for our Lord is with us, near us, all around us. Practicing His presence day and night is of greatest comfort to the people of God. It's our supreme secret, our deepest solace, our strongest weapon. The Lord is near, the Lord is here, our refuge and strength, a very present help in trouble.

Sir William Dobbie was a British war hero and devoted Christian who, during World War II, was given command of the Malta. Dobbie told the ill-prepared islanders that God was a very present help in trouble. And against all odds Malta did not fall. Allied battleships in its harbor were sitting ducks for the enemy, but the ships were never hit. A bomb fell through the roof of the village church, but it didn't go off. Nearly three hundred enemy planes were destroyed and six hundred others damaged. Allied forces in Malta threatened enemy supply lines and prevented Axis planes from reaching Europe. Dobbie's men said he possessed an inner calm impossible to understand. After the war he wrote a book about the "Miracle of Malta." He entitled his account *A Very Present Help.*

❋ I found that God was to me a Resource and a Helper to whom I could always turn; that He was, in fact, a very present help in trouble. That fact made all the difference to me.[90]—Lt. General Sir William Dobbie

62. Philippians 4:6

Don't worry about anything, but in everything, through prayer and petition with thanksgiving, let your requests be made known to God.

In his biography of Sidlow Baxter, E. A. Johnston relates a story about this verse. When Baxter was eighty-eight, he preached in Memphis, saying, "I was over in Scotland and at one point while there I slumped into a deep despondency. Everything seemed upsetting and frustrating and foreboding. . . . It seemed as though the promises of the Bible were like pie crust. Was it any use praying longer? I was having trouble with deafness. And along with that, tinnitus. Loud noises in both my ears day and night. . . . I went to bed weary with mental wrestling and frustration. And then, somewhere between night and morning, September 6th and 7th, something happened that changed everything. I heard no audible voice but someone had wakened me amid the curtains of the night; and was speaking within me. . . . He said, 'Sid! Sid! Are you forgetting Philippians 4, verses 6 and 7?' Those verses 6 and 7 perfectly match September 6 and 7. 'You've been forgetting the thanksgiving. Hand everything over to Me, Sid. And start praying again with thanksgiving. And start believing that what you ask for becomes yours. TRY IT, Sid. And if you do, Philippians 4:6 and 7 is all yours.'"

Baxter continued: "Philippians 4:6 and 7 was like an electric bulb turned on. And I saw everything with illuminating difference and clearness. . . . My whole nervous system had become relaxed. And as I prayed with thanksgiving—I could never forget it—the peace of God invaded my heart like a gentle zephyr."[91]

Ruth Bell Graham once told of laying awake at three o'clock in another country, worried about someone she loved who was trying hard to run away from God. As she later recalled, "Suddenly the Lord said to me, 'Quit studying the problems and start studying the promises.' Now God has never spoken to me audibly, but there is no mistaking when He speaks. So I turned on the light, got out my Bible, and the first verse that came to me was Philippians 4:6."

The two words that struck her were these: *with thanksgiving.*

"Suddenly I realized the missing ingredient in my prayers had been 'with thanksgiving.' So I put down my Bible and spent time worshipping Him for who He is and what He is. . . . I began to thank God for giving me this one I loved so dearly in the first place. I even thanked Him for the difficult spots which taught me so much. And you know what happened? It was as if suddenly someone turned on the lights in my mind and heart, and the little fears and worries which, like mice and cockroaches, had been nibbling away in the darkness, suddenly scuttled for cover."[92]

※ Those words, "in everything" are blessed. . . . The Bible here plainly commands us that "in everything" we should make our requests known to God.[93]—John R. Rice

63. Philippians 4:7

And the peace of God, which surpasses every thought,
will guard your hearts and your minds in Christ Jesus.

If you rejoice in the Lord, practice graciousness, practice God's nearness, cast your worries on Him, and pray with thanksgiving, the peace of God "shall garrison and mount guard over your hearts and minds in Christ Jesus" (Amplified Bible).

- **And**: The first word here is the conjunction "and," which connects this promise to the conditions previously mentioned.
- **The peace of God**: This isn't just the peace God gives; it's the peace He enjoys, His own internal dimensions of peace. It's the peace of Christ Himself, who said in John 14:27: "My peace I give to you."
- **Which surpasses every thought**: It's beyond our ability to understand it or to explain it to others. When we do as God commands here, we're promised an inner composure utterly unexplainable and inexplicable.
- **Will guard**: Paul used a Greek military term here, which meant to station sentries to protect, defend, and preserve an area.
- **Your hearts and minds**: Our emotions and our thoughts.
- **In Christ Jesus**: It's part of the birthright of those in an abiding relationship with Him.

In his book *Spiritual Depression,* Martyn Lloyd-Jones told of a Salvation Army worker and his wife, Mr. and Mrs. John George Carpenter, who had a radiant daughter dedicated to Asian missionary work. When she contracted typhoid, the Carpenters prayed earnestly but somehow felt they shouldn't pray for recovery. Their prayer was for God to heal her if it was His will. They prayed like this for six weeks, then the girl passed away. The morning she died, John said to his wife, "You know, I am aware of a strange and curious calm within." Mrs. Carpenter said, "I feel exactly the same. This must be the peace of God."

"And it was the peace of God," said Lloyd-Jones. "It was the peace of God keeping the heart and mind quiet in the sense that they could not upset the person. . . . They could not understand it, and that was the only explanation—'it must be the peace of God.' It was. Thank God for it. You and I cannot explain these things, they overpower us; but He is Almighty. With prayer and supplication and thanksgiving, therefore, let your requests be made known unto Him, and He, through his peace in Christ, will keep your heart and mind at rest and in peace."[94]

MEMORY TIP

Consider adding verses 8 and 9 to your memory work. It completes the thought. While verse 7 talks about the peace of God, verse 9 promises something even better—the God of peace.

❋ God the Father is called the God of Peace (Heb. 13:20). God the Son, the Prince of Peace (Isa. 9:6). God the Holy Ghost, the Spirit of Peace (Eph. 4:3).[95]—Thomas Watson

64. James 1:2

Consider it a great joy, my brothers, whenever you experience various trials.

The old translations say, "Count it all joy." The word *count* or *consider* is a Greek word meaning to think things through, to consider things mentally, to look at something from a different mind-set. The actual Greek term means "to make a decision about something after weighing all the facts and circumstances."

When believers have a series of reversals or difficulties, our first emotions and reactions may be painful; but we have divine resources, divine help, and divine truth to help us as we think it through and work it out in our minds. In so doing we'll come to a different conclusion about our problems than a non-Christian would.

I remember hearing my wife talk about her mother, Hilja, a wonderful Finnish-American who loved the Lord. On one occasion she received terrible news. It was like a blow in the stomach. But as Katrina remembers it, her mother took off her apron, left the house, and walked for what seemed like hours in the fields and lanes near her home in inland Maine, thinking things through, praying about it, and giving it to the Lord. When she returned, she was composed and better able to deal with the situation.

If we can think things through from the Lord's perspective, our feelings respond. We know that God intends to use these things for our good and for His glory, and we can count it all joy. I like the way the Phillips version puts this passage: *When all kinds of trials and temptations crowd into your lives my brothers, don't resent them as intruders, but welcome them as friends! Realize that they come to test your faith and to produce in you the quality of endurance.*

Joy Ridderhof, founder of Gospel Recordings, turned to James 1:2 again and again. In one of her autobiographical devotional books, she told of traveling in the South Pacific. "When I arrived in New Zealand I found that my one suitcase had been lost in transit. I remembered to 'count it all joy' and what do you think happened? My host and hostess who owned a department store completely outfitted me for my travel in cold New Zealand! Besides this my host asked for my ticket which just took me as far as Australia, and exchanged it for a round-the-world-ticket—a gift! When I arrived in Australia and needed to attend to the securing of visas for my stops in various countries, I found that to apply for entrance required exactly the sort of ticket I'd been given. . . . When I arrived in Sydney airport, there waiting for me right before my eyes was my lost bag . . . ! While we wait for His answers, let us 'count it all joy!'"[96]

※ [Count it all joy] is one of those Scripture paradoxes which nevertheless, the more we consider them will be found the more certainly true.[97]—William Gresley

65. James 1:3

*Knowing that the testing of your faith produces endur-
ance.*

"Counting it all joy" means looking at our problems not as isolated
incidents but in terms of God's chain reactions. The Lord works in
mysterious ways, and James strips away the covering so we can see the
machinery of His operation: *Consider it a great joy . . . whenever you experience various trials, knowing that the testing of your faith produces endurance. But endurance must do its complete work, so that you may be mature
and complete, lacking nothing.*

Notice the sequence: Various trials come to test our faith. The testing of our faith produces endurance and perseverance, and that results
in maturity. We see the same process outlined by the apostle Paul in
Romans 5: *We also rejoice in our afflictions, because we know that affliction produces endurance, endurance produces proven character, and proven
charter produces hope.*

Notice the key words. The term "testing" is akin to the idea of exercise. If faith never goes to the gym, it becomes flabby. As we encounter
trials, our faith is put to the test, exercised, put through its paces. As our
faith develops muscles, we become people of greater stamina and inner
strength. That gives us maturity and proven character.

Endurance is the ability to undergo a period of stress and strain with
the inner strength of Christ, emerging from it stronger than when we
entered. It's looking squarely into the face of discouraging circumstances
without despair. It's assuming that God is going to work all things for
good. It's acting as though it's already done though yet unseen. This
seems to be a quality the Lord values beyond almost all else. It's one of
His secret formulas in developing the chemistries of our Christian personalities:

Trials > Endurance/Perseverance > Maturity/Proven Character

From Charles Spurgeon's sermon on this verse.

"Look at the weather-beaten sailor, the man at home on the sea. He has a bronzed face and mahogany-colored flesh. He looks as tough as oak and as hardy as if made of iron. How different from us poor landsmen. He can go out to sea in any kind of weather; he has his sea legs on. How did he come to this strength? By doing business in great waters. He could not have become a hardy seaman by tarrying on shore. Now, trial works in the saints that spiritual hardihood which cannot be learned in ease. You may go to school forever, but you cannot learn endurance there: you may color your cheek with paint, but you cannot give it that ingrained brown which comes of stormy seas and howling winds."[98]

※ Sooner or later, the truth will be that God is now exercising His child—His consecrated child—in the ways of adult godliness . . . so that their powers of resistance might grow greater, and their character as men of God become stronger.[99]—J. I. Packer

66. James 1:4

But endurance must do its complete work, so that you may be mature and complete, lacking nothing.

This verse is a link in the chain connecting our worries (v. 3) with God's wisdom (v. 5). When facing trials of various kinds, we shouldn't view them as bad luck or as random misfortunes. They may be consequences of regrettable decisions or unavoidable debacles. They may appear as tragic accidents or be sent by Satan. But there is a Savior who embraced all our struggles while stretched on the crossbar of Calvary. He not only redeems our souls from sin but our circumstances from despair. He promises to wrest everything into conformity to His will and turn all things for good in our lives.

James 1:2–5 shows us how to manage problems from the perspective of Calvary. Jesus' death and resurrection enable us to "count it all joy" by understanding the process by which God produces people who bear the image of Christ. Our trials exercise our faith and build our spiritual muscles. The resulting stamina gives us greater endurance, leading to maturity.

That doesn't mean it's easy. Anyone can say, "Count it all joy!" But the old British preacher, Joseph Parker, prayed honestly when he said, "Almighty God, we have tried to count it all joy when we have fallen into divers temptations, but we have failed in the attempt. It is hard to count it joy. . . . How can we count it all joy when we are in the midst of the tremendous assault?"

But he went on in his prayer to say, "Train us in this high-mindedness, this noble reverence, this rational and religious submission. This only can be done at the Cross of Jesus Christ Thy Son; there is no other school in which we can learn such wisdom."[100]

When I was growing up, my Aunt Louise owned a metal fabricating factory; and in those days before OSHA (the Occupational Safety and Health Administration), I wandered rather freely among the men and machines. Forklifts and overhead cranes swung steel through the air like flyers on a trapeze. Metal was unrolled, crushed and crunched into useful shapes, then plunged into acid baths before heading to the delivery trucks. To a boy like me, it was loud, confusing, and a little frightening. But I'm glad I saw what goes into the pipes that bring clear drinking water into my kitchen sink.

This passage in James 1 is a tour of the industrial park where God forms and fashions us into pipelines for the living waters. We're under construction, but the testing of our faith produces endurance, leading to maturity; and through it all we become channels of blessings.

※ My old eyes get dimmer. The specialist says the light will fade altogether. So I gird myself for darkness, quote James 1:2 to 4, shout Hallelujah and go on.[101]—Salvation Army hero, Samuel Logan Brengle, facing old age and blindness

67. James 1:5

Now if any of you lacks wisdom, he should ask God, who
gives to all generously and without criticizing, and it will
be given to him.

The God of Israel once offered the king of Israel anything he wanted.
Young King Solomon requested wisdom, and God bestowed it freely.
Here in James 1, we're given the same offer. But notice the context. The
"wisdom" God offers is connected with the "various trials" of verse 2,
the "testing of our faith" of verse 3, and our need for maturity in verse 4.

In times of strain, we need to see the sovereign, providential ways
of God, and we need the calmness of His peace. We need the ability to
make right decisions and give judicious advice. Wisdom is the God-given
ability to say and do the right thing, in the right way, at the right time,
with the right tone, and for the right reasons.

This verse assures us that God willingly gives such wisdom without
scolding us for not having it ourselves. It's important, however, to ask in
faith without doubting. "For the doubter is like the surging sea, driven
and tossed by the wind" (v. 6).

The devotional writer Hannah Whitall Smith said about this verse,
"A wavering Christian is a Christian who trusts in the love of God one
day and doubts it the next, and who is alternately happy or miserable
accordingly . . . driven to and fro by every wind of doctrine. . . . You
would suppose that even the most ignorant child of God would know
without telling that this sort of experience is all wrong, and that to waver
in one's faith after such a fashion was one of the things most dishonoring
to the Lord. . . . A wavering faith is not only disloyal to God, but it is a
source of untold misery to ourselves and cannot in any way advance our
spiritual interests."[102]

God wants to advance our spiritual interests. Don't waver or worry;
just ask for wisdom and trust Him to give it as needed.

Want to live in the town of Wisdom? In Southwest Montana, there's a little town (population about one hundred) with that name. I'd like to pay a visit there, wouldn't you? Wisdom is situated along the trail explored by Lewis and Clark, and it was named Wisdom because it grew up beside the river that Meriwether Lewis dubbed "Wisdom River" in honor of the purported wisdom of President Thomas Jefferson.

Perhaps we can't live there geographically, but we can live there biblically. When we dwell in Wisdom and drink from the waters of Wisdom River, we remain calm, make good decisions, and count it all joy.

※ There are three points to be noted (in James 1:5). . . . One is the great deficiency in the average Christian character—wisdom; another is the great means of supplying it—ask; and the third is the great guarantee of the supply—the giving God.[103]—Alexander Maclaren

68. 1 Thessalonians 5:16

Rejoice always!

Our next three verses, 1 Thessalonians 5:16–18, comprise one of the shortest paragraphs of the Bible, yet this sliver of a passage has the ability drastically to improve our temperaments. It's no accident they appear near the end of 1 Thessalonians. Thumb through Paul's letters in the Bible; notice how often he grows succinct and aphoristic near the end of his books, as he runs out of parchment. I love the pithy wisdom that marks the conclusions of his letters. At the end of 1 Thessalonians, for example, he starts "bullet-pointing" his advice like this:

> [16] *Rejoice always!*
>
> [17] *Pray constantly.*
>
> [18] *Give thanks in everything, for this is God's will for you in Christ Jesus.*
>
> [19] *Don't stifle the Spirit.*
>
> [20] *Don't despise prophecies,*
>
> [21] *But test all things. Hold on to what is good.*
>
> [22] *Stay away from every form of evil.*

Verse 16 ("Rejoice always!") is the shortened form of Philippians 4:4 ("Rejoice in the Lord always. I will say it again: Rejoice!") The Greek word refers to the uplifting, ongoing, cheerfulness of the Christian. Joy is the helium of the heart that makes us airborne. It's the corklike quality of our souls that keeps us buoyant.

Sadness and sorrow befall us in life. Tears come. Disasters strike. But by and large, the *default attitude* of the believer is the joy of the Lord. That's the natural "setting" of the Christlike person. Uplifting, outgoing cheerfulness. Gladness.

I once read of a man who smelled good wherever he was and whatever he was doing. His very skin seemed to exude a pleasant fragrance. He worked in a perfume factory, and he breathed the aromas every day.

They filtered into his clothing, penetrated his skin, and even filled his lungs. He became a walking perfumery.

That should be happening to us. As biblical joy pervades one's personality, it puts a smile on the face, a sparkle in the eye, a bounce in the step, a warmth in the voice, a confidence in the heart, and a composure in the demeanor. It should exude from us like the essence of the Savior. The joy of the Lord is the strength of our lives.

Rejoice sometimes? Rejoice always!

There's no excuse for not memorizing this verse. It's the shortest in the Bible. As a child, I was told that John 11:35 ("Jesus wept") was the Bible's smallest verse. That *is* the shortest verse in the English Bible. But in the Greek New Testament, 1 Thessalonians 5:16 is even shorter. In a sense we have *two* shortest verses in the Bible. In the Greek, it is "Rejoice always," and in our English Bibles, it's "Jesus wept." Quite a contrast, isn't it—weeping and rejoicing? But how appropriate! Because Jesus wept, we can rejoice. Because He bears our sorrows, we experience His joy.

※ God pays in joy that is fireproof, famine-proof and devil-proof.[104]
—Billy Sunday

69. 1 Thessalonians 5:17

Pray constantly.

Pray constantly is midway through a trilogy of tiny, personality-altering verses at the end of 1 Thessalonians. Millions have memorized this verse from the King James Version, as "Pray without ceasing," wondering if it's really possible to do that. It *is* . . . when we understand:

Prayer is a practice to cultivate. To *pray constantly* means prayer is recurrent, something we keep doing incessantly and frequently, a perpetual pattern, not constantly occurring but consistently recurring. If we read through 1 Thessalonians, by the time we get to this verse, we'll have noticed several prior references to the habit. Paul began the book saying, "We always thank God for all of you, remembering you constantly in our prayers." In chapter 2 he said, "We constantly thank God, because . . . you received the message." He added in chapter 3, "We pray earnestly night and day to see you face to face." Paul wasn't literally on his knees around the clock, but his prayers were frequent and recurrent.

Prayer is a presence to enjoy. Prayer isn't just a pattern; it's a Presence. If you've traveled alone, especially overseas, you may know about hotel loneliness. Some people live with lonesomeness all the time. A constant awareness of God's presence is a shaft of light in a lonely room. Jesus Himself testified to this on two occasions in the fourth Gospel. In John 8:16, He said, "*I am not alone*, but I and the Father who sent Me judge together." And in the upper room just before His arrest and crucifixion, He said, "The time is coming—indeed it's here now—when you will be scattered, each one going his own way, leaving me alone. Yet *I am not alone* because the Father is with me" (John 16:31–32 NLT, emphasis mine in both verses).

When we cultivate a consciousness and subconsciousness of God's abiding presence, it becomes natural to speak to Him spontaneously through the day. We learn to pray as we walk on the greenways and drive down the highways. We start and close the day with a word of prayer.

We pause to pray before meals and after meetings. We never endeavor anything of significance without breathing a word of prayer or praise.

That's a practice to cultivate and a Presence to enjoy. And that's how we pray without ceasing.

In his classic book *With Christ in the School of Prayer,* Andrew Murray draws a line between this verse and Hebrews 7:25, which says Christ "ever lives to make intercession" for us. "It is ... the sight of the ever-praying Christ as our life that enables us to pray without ceasing," wrote Murray. "Because His priesthood is the prayer of an endless life ... praying without ceasing can become to us nothing less than the life-joy of heaven."[105]

❋ "Rejoice evermore: pray without ceasing; in everything give thanks." Borne up between the never-ceasing joy and never-ceasing praise, never-ceasing prayer is the manifestation of the power of the eternal life.[106]—Andrew Murray

70. 1 Thessalonians 5:18

*Give thanks in everything, for this is God's will for you
in Christ Jesus.*

In medicine the smallest germs can wreak the most havoc, and the tiniest pills can pack the biggest punch. First Thessalonians 5:16–18 is a wafer-thin paragraph that has an outsized effect on our personalities. It can cure our irritability, lighten our depression, lessen our anxiety, and improve our dispositions. It's one of the most psychologically potent passages in the Bible; and, when memorized and practiced, it can alter our attitude at any given time.

In staccato-like style, the apostle Paul tells us to be joyful, prayerful, and thankful. And all three verses are all-pervading: Rejoice always! Pray constantly. Give thanks in everything.

Rejoice. Pray. Give thanks. Always. Constantly. Everything.

At fourteen words, 1 Thessalonians 5:18 is the longest verse in the trilogy. It's the counterpart to another of our memory verses, Romans 8:28, which says, "We know that all things work together for the good of those who love God." Because all things work together for good, we can give thanks in everything.

The Bible doesn't tell us to be thankful *for* everything. Some things are bad in their very nature. There are no examples of biblical heroes thanking God for evil events or demonic attacks. But we can be thankful *in* all things, for God has promised to turn them for good.

Many psychologists believe we are born with preset happiness levels. Just as everyone has a different body, so we have different personalities. Some are sanguine; others have a melancholy streak. Dr. Robert Emmons of the University of California Davis has demonstrated there is one way to adjust those preprogrammed, inborn personality settings. It's by developing the habit of consciously giving thanks in the midst of whatever circumstances we may face.

"We discovered scientific proof that when people regularly engage in the systematic cultivation of gratitude, they experience a variety of measurable benefits: psychological, physical, and interpersonal," wrote Dr. Emmons. "The evidence on gratitude contradicts the widely held view that all people have a 'set-point' of happiness that cannot be reset by any known means."[107]

This is the advice issued 2,000 years ago in 1 Thessalonians 5:18. *Give thanks in everything, for this is God's will for you in Christ Jesus.*

MEMORY TIP

In developing lifelong habits of Scripture memory, most people find pleasure in memorizing passages rather than individual verses. When we memorize a passage like 1 Thessalonians 5:16–18, we're learning a longer block of Scripture, but the progression from verse to verse is logical, easy to absorb, and simpler to remember. As we memorize subsequent verses, we automatically review earlier ones. And we learn the Bible contextually. Learning a verse in its context enables us to interpret and apply it more accurately. Consider expanding your memory work in this chapter. Verses 12–24 provides a baker's dozen of great verses that are among the most psychologically powerful in the epistles.

※ We can't always give thanks FOR everything, but we can always give thanks IN everything.[108]—Ruth Bell Graham

FAITH:

Trusting God and Resting in His Word

71. Ephesians 2:8

For by grace you are saved through faith, and this is not from yourselves; it is God's gift.

Suppose we took a microphone to the mall and asked people, "Do you believe you're going to heaven when you die?" Many would say, "I hope so. I'm trying to live a good life. I'm trying to be a good person." Ephesians 2 begs to differ. We can never get to heaven by our own merits or on the basis of what we are trying to do.

This chapter begins by reviewing our past. We were dead in our trespasses and sins (v. 1), walking according to the world (v. 2), carrying out our fleshly desires, and facing the wrath of God (v. 3). But God, who exudes abundant love and mercy, made us alive by grace (vv. 4–5) and has given us an eternal inheritance in Christ (vv. 6–7).

Verse 8 punches home this fact; it's the Bible's premier text on the subject: *For by grace you are saved through faith, and this is not from yourselves; it is God's gift.*

When Jesus died on the cross, He shouted three words that ring through the ages and echo from the heavens to the four corners of earth: *It is finished!* When we think about salvation, we don't think of the word *do* but of the word *done*. It isn't righteous acts we do or works of charity we perform. It's not a matter of living a good life or hoping that our altruistic actions outweigh our selfish ones. It's a matter of what Jesus Christ has *done* for us on the cross. We are saved by grace.

Ephesians 2:8–10 was the text for an unusual tag-team sermon by James Spurgeon and his grandson Charles. The younger Spurgeon, who was just beginning to preach, had been invited to speak at a certain church, but his train was late. James stood up and started the sermon in his place, choosing Ephesians 2:8–9 as his text. When Charles arrived, James said, "Here comes my grandson. He can preach the Gospel better than I can, but you cannot preach a better Gospel, can you?"

Charles mounted the pulpit and began where his grandfather had left off. A few minutes later, when Charles was speaking about human sinfulness, James whispered, "I know most about that." Charles sat down, and James took over and finished that point; then he turned the pulpit back over to his grandson. As he resumed, Charles could hear his grandfather behind him, "Good! Good! Tell them that again, Charles."

For the rest of his life, whenever Charles read or preached from Ephesians 2, there came to him with recurring force his grandfather's words, "Tell them that again, Charles! Tell them that again."[109]

※ Of the things which I have spoken unto you these many years, this is the sum. Within the circle of these words (Ephesians 2:8) my theology is contained, so far as it refers to the salvation of men.[110]—Charles Haddon Spurgeon

72. Ephesians 2:9

Not from works, so that no one can boast.

As the Reformation began spreading over Europe, authorities in Amsterdam sought to limit its effect. When a Protestant rally was announced on an estate outside the city, the city gates were shut to prevent people from attending. But many people swam out through the canals or escaped through small passages in the wall. Multitudes forced their way out when the gates were opened to let the milkmaids into the fields for the morning milking. By eleven o'clock the city rulers gave in, and the gates were opened for all to attend the meeting. More than five thousand people gathered to hear Pieter Gabriel preach a four-hour sermon from Ephesians 2:8–9: "For by grace you are saved through faith, and this is not from yourselves; it is God's gift—not from works, so that no one can boast." It helped establish the Reformation in Holland.[111]

"Justification by grace through faith" was the rallying cry of the Reformation, but what does it mean to say we're not saved by works?

It means we can never earn our way into eternal life by good deeds, mission trips, winning smiles, pleasant personalities, study habits, worship attendance, baptism, church membership, getting along with others, volunteering at mercy centers, helping the homeless, caring for unwanted youngsters, writing checks, giving money to worthy causes, keeping the law, being a good neighbor, being a good citizen, wearing religious symbols, telling the truth, uttering mantras, performing acts of heroism, doing random acts of kindness, or giving someone our parking space.

Could we build a ladder to the moon with hammer and nails? Could we tunnel through the earth with pick and shovel? Could we swim across the Pacific with mask and fins? The distance to heaven is far greater than to the moon, through the earth, or across the sea. The chasm between us and God is bridged only by the cross of Christ. It's "not by works of righteousness that we had done, but according to His mercy" that we are saved (Titus 3:5). Not by works, lest anyone should boast.

Lord, we confess our numerous faults,
How great our guilt has been!
Foolish and vain were all our thoughts,
And all our lives were sin.

'Tis not by works of righteousness
Which our own hands have done;
But we are saved by sovereign grace
Abounding through His Son.

Raised from the dead we live anew;
And, justified by grace,
We shall appear in glory too,
And see our Father's face.
—Isaac Watts

❅ Indeed this is one of the greatest mysteries in the world—namely, that a righteousness that resides with a Person in heaven should justify me, a sinner on earth.[112]—John Bunyan

73. Ephesians 2:10

For we are His creation—created in Christ Jesus for good works, which God prepared ahead of time so that we should walk in them.

In memorizing Ephesians 2:8–9, it's vital to learn verse 10, too, for this balances out the Bible's teaching about good works. We can never be saved *by doing* good works, but we are saved *to do* good works. The New International Version says, "For we are God's workmanship, created in Christ Jesus to do good works, which God prepared in advance for us to do."

This is an incredible verse because it tells us that while good works aren't the cause of our salvation, they are the result of it; and God has even planned in advance what those good works will be in your life and mine.

Titus 3:4–8 make the same point: "He saved us—not by works of righteousness that we had done, but according to His mercy. . . . I want you to insist on these things, so that those who have believed God might be careful to devote themselves to good works."

When you study the history of the world, you'll find that Christians have always been at the forefront of benevolence, social reform, education, hospitality, and medical care. Jesus told us to let our light shine before others that they might see our good works and glorify our Father who is in heaven (Matt. 5:16). He said when we visit the prisoners and feed the hungry and help the oppressed, it's as though we were doing it for Him (Matt. 25:45).

We are His workmanship, created in Christ Jesus to do His good works in this world.

Even knowledgeable believers will be amazed at how many of our present institutions and values reflect a Christian origin. Not only countless individual lives but civilization itself was transformed by Jesus Christ. In the ancient world, His teachings elevated brutish standards of morality, halted infanticide, enhanced human life, emancipated women, abolished slavery, inspired charities and relief organizations, created hospitals, established orphanages, and founded schools.

In medieval times, Christianity almost single-handedly kept classical culture alive through recopying manuscripts, building libraries, moderating warfare through truce days, and providing dispute arbitration. It was Christians who invented colleges and universities, dignified labor as a divine vocation, and extended the light of civilization to barbarians on the frontiers.

In the modern era, Christian teaching, properly expressed, advanced science, instilled concepts of political and social and economic freedom, fostered justice, and provided the greatest single source of inspiration for the magnificent achievements in art, architecture, music, and literature that we treasure to this present day. . . . No other religion, philosophy, teaching, nation, movement—whatever—has so changed the world for the better as Christianity has done.[113]—Paul Maier in *How Christianity Changed the World* by Alvin J. Schmidt

※ There are two kinds of good works; some precede and others follow justification. The former merely appear to be good and effectual; the latter are really good.[114]—Martin Luther

74. Galatians 2:20

I have been crucified with Christ; and I no longer live,
but Christ lives in me. The life I now live in the flesh,
I live by faith in the Son of God, who loved me and gave
Himself for me.[115]

This is a verse I memorized during my college days. I've been mulling over it for forty years, but I have yet to plumb its depths. In simplest fashion it seems to present three configurations to the Christian life.

1. **The relinquished life.** We've been crucified with Christ, which means we've come to the old rugged cross and gazed on the dying form of one who suffered there for us. Deeply moved, we turn aside from the kind of life we once lived and take our stand at Calvary. When James Calvert went out as a missionary to the cannibals of the Fiji Islands, the captain of the ship sought to turn him back. "You will lose your life and the lives of those with you if you go among such savages," he cried. Calvert only replied, "We died before we came here." There comes a time when we must stop living for our own plans in life, give up ownership of ourselves, and say, "Your will be done in me."

2. **The exchanged life.** We no longer live; Christ lives in us. None of us can ever live the Christian life in our own strength. None of us can resist temptation by our own determination. None of us can love as we should just by our own efforts. The Christian life is the Lord Jesus daily living His life through us by means of the Holy Spirit.

3. **The trusting life.** The life we live in the flesh, we live by faith in the Son of God who loved us and give Himself for us. We're saved by faith, we work by faith, and we walk with Him day by day, enjoying His presence and fully trusting His promises.

During my college years in South Carolina, I asked my pastor, Dr. H. Edwin Young, if he could tell me the secret of Christian service. He said, "You have to die to yourself every day. You have to put 220 volts to yourself every day—Galatians 2:20. 'I am crucified with Christ.'"

Someone asked George Müller, the secret of his victorious Christian life. He replied: "There came a day when George Müller died, utterly died! No longer did his own desires, preferences, and tastes come first. He knew that from then on Christ must be all in all."

This sign appeared in the window of a dry-cleaning and dying business: "We dye to live, we live to dye; the more we dye, the more we live; and the more we live, the more we dye."

※ When God calls a man, he bids him come and die.[116]—Dietrich Bonhoeffer

75. Colossians 3:15

*And let the peace of the Messiah, to which you were
called in one body, control your hearts. Be thankful.*

I learned this verse in the New International Version, which says,
"Let the peace of Christ rule in your hearts, since as members of one body
you were called to peace. And be thankful." The word *rule* or *control* is
the translation of a Greek term found only here in the New Testament. It
literally means "to sit as umpire" or "to arbitrate." As we grow in Christ,
the inner peace of Christ will act as an umpire when envy, anger, and
anxiety come calling.

Peace can be defined as God-given tranquility. It's the ability to be
patient instead of panicky, to be mature instead of impulsive, to keep our
cool when others are losing theirs. It's a quality that few of us come by
naturally, but it came perfectly to Jesus.

In Luke 4, Jesus was asked to preach in His hometown of Nazareth.
After reading His text in Isaiah 61, He closed the book and announced
that He Himself was the one of whom Isaiah was speaking. Isaiah's
majestic words, written seven hundred years before, amounted to a specific prediction about the hometown boy who stood before them now.
The Nazarenes, Jesus implied, were seeing the fulfillment of Messianic
prophecy before their very eyes.

It triggered a riot. Thinking Jesus was speaking blasphemously, the
worshippers exploded in fury and indignation. The crowd was on its feet,
and angry hands grabbed Jesus and shoved Him out of the synagogue,
pushing Him, pulling Him toward a nearby cliff. They intended to kill
Him on the spot.

But as Luke laconically puts it, "He passed right through and went
on His way" (Luke 4:30). We don't know if this was a miracle or not.
But we have the distinct impression that Jesus was unruffled, steady,
composed, and self-possessed. I've often visualized Jesus passing calmly
through these walls of liquid indignation like the Israelites through the
Red Sea. There was about Him an authoritative calmness.

That's the peace He possesses; that's the composure He imparts.

The last phrase of the verse says, "Be thankful." As the *Bible Knowledge Commentary* puts it, "An attitude of gratitude contributes to an enjoyment of spiritual tranquility, whereas grumbling makes for inner agitation."[117] Colossians 5:15–17 is the climax to Paul's teaching about unity in the church. He begins the chapter by telling us to set our minds on things above (v. 2), to put to death disruptive attitudes like anger, malice, slander, and filthy language (vv. 5–8). He warns against lying and racial prejudice (vv. 9–11). Instead we're to put on compassion, kindness, humility, and love, which is the perfect bond of unity (vv. 12–14). We're to let the peace of Christ rule in our hearts.

※ The real strength and majesty of the soul of man is calmness, the manifestation of strength, the peace of God ruling.[118]—Frederick W. Robertson

76. Colossians 3:16

Let the message about the Messiah dwell richly among you, teaching and admonishing one another in all wisdom, and singing psalms, hymns, and spiritual songs, with gratitude in your hearts to God.

Just as John 3:16 provides the core of the gospel, Colossians 3:16 provides the core of worship. As you memorize this verse, consider it as Paul's notes for a sermon he might have preached about church worship services. Here are his points:

1. **Worship includes biblical exposition.** Paul was concerned the message of Christ be richly presented through teaching and admonition. The word *richly* means "abundantly, in great measure, in large amounts."

2. **Worship involves "one another."** Teaching and admonition aren't just pulpit-to-pew affairs. We teach and admonish one another. I'm reminded of another 3:16: Malachi 3:16: "At that time those who feared the LORD spoke to one another. The LORD took notice and listened."

3. **Singing is a big part of worship, and . . .**

4. **Variety in musical styles is welcomed.** We're to sing out God's Word in psalms, hymns, and spiritual songs. Psalms are Bible-based praises that are solid, deep, echoing the words of Scripture (especially the book of Psalms). Hymns are rich and sturdy songs that stand the test of time. Spiritual songs are lighter, livelier expressions of our faith and worship.

5. **Worship rises on the wings of thanksgiving.** Even though Paul ended the previous verse with the words "Be thankful," he came right back in this verse to repeat the thought with the phrase "with gratitude."

6. **Worship includes prayer.** Notice the last two words of the verse: "to God."

7. **Worship should engage both mind and emotions.**
   Colossians 3:16 tells us to admonish with all *wisdom* (our minds) and to sing with our hearts (our emotions). This recalls our Lord's words in John 4, that God desires us to worship Him in spirit and in truth.

As you memorize these verses, you may get them confused with the previous passage from Ephesians 5. Paul wrote Ephesians and Colossians at the same time and from the same cell, and he expressed similar sentiments in both. But there are significant differences. Ephesians 5 tells us that when we're filled with the Spirit, we'll be speaking to one another in psalms, hymns, and spiritual songs. Colossians 3:16 says the same will be true when the Word of God dwells richly among us. Think of your automobile. Your engine needs both fuel and spark. For the engine of worship, the fuel is the Word of God, and the fullness of the Holy Spirit gives the spark. Biblical teaching without spiritual power produces cold orthodoxy. Spiritual excitement without the Word of God promotes religious fanaticism. Put both together, and you've got biblical worship.

※ The rule is . . . that we turn each truth that we learn *about* God into a matter of mediation *before* God, leading to prayer and praise *to* God.[119]—J. I. Packer

77. Colossians 3:17

*And whatever you do, in word or in deed, do everything
in the name of the Lord Jesus, giving thanks to God the
Father through Him.*

I'd like to take this opportunity to introduce you to the *"whatever
you do"* verses. These are sweeping commands spanning all our words,
thoughts, attitudes, and actions, designed to make us living doxologies.
There are two such verses here in Colossians 3.

- **Whatever you do**, in word or deed, do everything in the
  name of the Lord Jesus, giving thanks to God the Father
  through Him (v. 17).
- **Whatever you do**, do it enthusiastically, as something done
  for the Lord and not for men (v. 23).

I'm intrigued by the phrase in verse 17: "in the name of the Lord
Jesus." That means we should do everything as though Jesus Himself
were doing it. Our every word should be as though Jesus were speaking
it.

Recently I had a medical procedure requiring anesthesia. The hospital wanted to know if I had a durable power of attorney, and they asked
who would make decisions in my name should a crisis arise. The person
who acts in my name does so with full legal authority as though I myself
were making the decision.

This verse tells us that whatever we *say* in life, we're to say it as
though Christ were saying it. Whatever we *do* in life, we're to do as
though Christ were doing it. Whatever we do in word or deed, we're to
do in the name of the Lord Jesus.

Furthermore, we're to do it with thanksgiving.

In Christian living, the small things we do are often bigger than
the large things we accomplish; the Lord delights in small things. But
whether small or large, let's do it all in the name of Christ for the glory
of God. That's our calling.

- Commit to the LORD whatever you do, and your plans will succeed. (Prov. 16:3 NIV)
- Plan carefully what you do, and whatever you do will turn out right. (Prov. 4:26 GNT)
- Work hard at whatever you do. (Eccles. 9:10 GNT)
- Do faithfully whatever you do. (3 John 5 NKJV)
- Whatever you do, do it enthusiastically, as something done for the Lord and not for men, knowing that you will receive the reward of an inheritance from . . . the Lord Christ. (Col. 3:23–24)
- Whatever you do, in word or in deed, do everything in the name of the Lord Jesus, giving thanks to God the Father through Him. (Col. 3:17)
- Remember that God is going to judge you for whatever you do. (Eccles. 11:9 GNT)
- Therefore, whether you eat or drink, or whatever you do, do everything for God's glory. (1 Cor. 10:31)[120]

※ We can do no great things, only small things with great love.[121]
—Mother Teresa

78. Romans 1:16

For I am not ashamed of the gospel, because it is God's
power for salvation to everyone who believes, first to the
Jew, and also to the Greek.

There's not another preacher in Christian history like George
Whitefield, who could stand on a tombstone and preach for an hour,
keeping vast crowds mesmerized with his wind-borne voice, which could
sometimes be heard a mile away. On one occasion, however, he was almost
daunted. He'd been invited to preach at a Whitsuntide fair in Marylebone
Fields. Whitefield and his wife, Elizabeth, arrived after dark, finding a
confusing scene of fighting and frivolity. Boxing booths were featuring
bare-fisted fights, surrounded by gambling booths and gin sellers.

When George, only twenty-seven at the time, climbed into a make-
shift pulpit and began preaching, the crowd turned on him. Boxers
left their rings, not bothering to put on their shirts or conceal their fists.
He paused mid-sentence, fearing a riot. Feeling a tug on his garment, he
looked down at his wife, Elizabeth, who said plainly, "George, play the
man for God."

With a surge of courage and compassion, he called out across the
fairground, "I am not ashamed of the gospel of Christ, for it is the power
of God until salvation to everyone who believes." Throwing his hands
into the air with an expansive gesture, he was alarmed to feel the platform wobble beneath him. Rocks and eggs flew toward him, and one
rogue tried to stab him with a sword. Still he preached from Romans
1:16 until souls were saved and a foothold for Christ was carved out in
the region.

As you read the prologue of Romans, which presents the theme and thesis of the book, notice Paul's three "I" statements in verses 14–16. They provide a powerful outline about witnessing:

- *I am obligated* (v. 14). Once we have met Jesus as Savior, we have an obligation to tell someone else what we've discovered.
- *I am eager* (v. 15). We don't just share our message out of obligation but out of excitement. We can't wait to share the good news.
- *I am unashamed* (v. 16). We aren't going to be intimidated by a hostile world or shamed into silence. We are the community of the unashamed.

For I am not ashamed of the gospel, because it is God's power for salvation to everyone who believes, first to the Jew, and also to the Greek.

※ The gospel will save the lost. Nothing else can do it. Nothing else is doing it. Nothing else has done it. Nothing else shall do it. "The gospel . . . is the power of God unto salvation, to everyone that believeth." The gospel convicts of sin, the gospel converts the soul. It is by the foolishness of preaching the gospel that men, women, and children are brought out of darkness into light, out of damnation into salvation, out of death into life, out of hell into heaven.[122]—Hyman Appelman

79. Romans 1:17

For in it God's righteousness is revealed from faith to
faith, just as it is written: The righteous will live by
faith.

In memorizing Romans 1:16–17, you have the whole book of Romans in digest form. These verses, coming at the end of Paul's magnificent prologue to Romans, summarize the theme and thesis of this book. Verses 16 and 17 provide the essential vocabulary of the Christian dictionary. As you read these two verses, underline these words:

- Gospel—The good news of Jesus Christ.
- God—The source of life, hope, forgiveness, and justification.
- Power—The omnipotence of heaven is packed into this message.
- Salvation—Deliverance from sin, death, despair, and hell.
- Everyone—The scope of the gospel is universal in its offer.
- Believes—The condition and requirement for justification.
- Righteousness—The state of being made right with God.
- Revealed—This message can't be discovered from below; it had to be revealed from above.
- Faith—This term occurs three times in verse 17, explaining the word *believes* in verse 16.

In the gospel Paul asserts, God's righteousness is revealed. That is, He tells us how we can share His righteousness and be restored into good standing with Him.

Martin Luther suggested that the phrase "from faith to faith" means that justification is entirely by faith. It is by faith from first to last.

As a final note, when we memorize the phrase, "The righteous will live by faith," we are memorizing a text that occurs four times in the Bible. You may want to look up the other three references as an aid to memorization: Habakkuk 2:4; Galatians 3:11; Hebrews 10:38.

This was Martin Luther's great Reformation verse. As a young monk, trying through asceticism and self-mortification to find peace with God, he was challenged by his mentor, Johann von Staupitz, to study and teach the book of Romans. He didn't get far before being stumped by verse 17, puzzling day after day over the meaning of the phrase "the righteousness of God." He finally realized it referred to the righteousness that God freely gives those who believe in him. We cannot be justified by our own merits; we're justified through faith on the basis of Christ's work on the cross. This insight lit up Luther's mind like a floodlight, and he began preaching it as the core of the gospel. Within a few years, the truth of Romans 1:17 swept over the world and changed the course of history.

※ The righteousness of God must not be understood as that righteousness by which (a person) is righteous in himself, but as that righteousness by which we are made righteous (justified) by Him, and this happens through faith in the Gospel.[123]—Martin Luther

80. Psalm 56:3

When I am afraid, I will trust in You.

Nine words and ten syllables. About the same length as your phone number. But what a life-changing sentence to learn and live! Notice the opening word—not *if* but *when*. Fear—in its various forms—besets us every day. And notice what Psalm 56:3 doesn't say:

- When afraid, I will panic or fall to pieces.
- When afraid, I will grow depressed and give up.
- When I am afraid, I will run and hide.

It says: "When I am afraid, I will trust in You"—in Your providence, in Your promises, in Your protection, in Your power, in Your peace. Faith is being confident that God's positives are greater than our negatives, and that His providence is overshadowing our lives. Faith in a faithful God is the only lasting antidote for debilitating fear.

In 1996 my friend Dana Thompson had trouble walking; and, following a trip to the emergency room, she was scheduled for a cardiac cauterization. But something went wrong during the procedure, and Dana woke up surrounded by frenetic activity and by the loud, windy chopping of helicopter wings. She was being airlifted to a medical center in Birmingham.

She was scared not only because she realized something was obviously wrong with her but also because she'd never been on a helicopter before and the weather was bad. "I was just shaking with fear," she said, "but I realized my fearful state wasn't honoring God or serving as a good testimony to the medical workers. I wracked my brain for a Bible verse to calm me down, but I could only think of one—*When I am afraid, I will trust in You.*

"I quoted that verse over and over in my mind as I looked down through the window and saw the houses and streets below. The ride was bumpy, but I started praying Psalm 56:3 to Him. My shaking and fretful trembling ceased and was replaced by a warmth and peace. I reassured the workers on the chopper that it was going to be all right, and I settled down to enjoy a God's-eye view of the countryside despite the conditions. Whatever happened, I knew, God had it covered."

When the chopper arrived at the medical center in Birmingham, a renowned cardiologist performed open-heart surgery. Dana wasn't able to thank the doctor at the time because he left immediately on a trip. But later she sent him a thank-you note thanking him and quoting Psalm 56:3.[124]

❊ There is nothing like faith to help at a pinch; faith dissolves doubts as the sun drives away the mists. . . . At what time, said the good man, I am afraid, I will trust in thee.[125]—John Bunyan

81. Psalm 4:8

I will both lie down and sleep in peace, for You alone,
LORD, make me live in safety.

The Psalms contain soothing verses about rest and sleep. Psalm 3, for example, was written while King David fled from his rebellious son Absalom; yet in verse 5, he said, "I lie down and sleep; I wake again because the LORD sustains me." Psalm 127:2 says, "Certainly He gives sleep to the one He loves." Psalm 23:2 says, "He lets me lie down in green pastures," and Psalm 121 reminds us that the keeper of Israel does not slumber or sleep. Since the Lord knows when we lie down (Ps. 139:3), we can sleep in peace, for He alone makes us dwell in safety (Ps. 4:8).

Psalm 4:8 is particularly easy to memorize because it's short, and it comes at the end of an unusual bedtime prayer. David sounds agitated at the beginning of this psalm, and many scholars believe it, too, was written during Absalom's rebellion. Notice how many people David addressed in these eight verses, as if turning to one person after another.

He began by praying to God in verses 1–2 ("Answer me"). Verses 2–3 addressed his enemies ("How long will you love what is worthless?"). In verses 4–5, he spoke to himself, reminding himself to calm down and not be sinfully agitated in bed. In the last three verses, he reverted to prayer again, admitting that his advisors were giving him nothing but bad news; yet, he said, he felt great inner joy and could *lie down and sleep, for You alone, LORD, make me live in safety.*

In this way Psalm 4:8 represents a great declaration of faith. Sometimes the greatest demonstration of faith isn't in moving mountains; it's in turning down the covers.

Psalm 4

Answer me when I call, God, who vindicates me.
You freed me from affliction; be gracious to me
and hear my prayer.
How long, exalted men, will my honor be insulted?
How long will you love what is worthless and pursue a lie?
Know that the LORD has set apart the faithful for Himself;
The LORD will hear when I call to Him.
Be angry and do not sin;
On your bed, reflect in your heart and be still.
Offer sacrifices in righteousness and trust in the LORD.
Many are saying, "Who can show us anything good?"
Look on us with favor, LORD.
You have put more joy in my heart
than they have when their grain and new wine abound.
I will both lie down and sleep in peace,
For You alone, LORD, make me live in safety.

✻ How many of our sleepless hours might be traced to our untrusting
and disordered minds. They slumber sweetly whom faith rocks to sleep.
No pillow so soft as a promise; no coverlet so warm as an assured interest in Christ.[126]—Charles Haddon Spurgeon

82. Hebrews 11:6

Now without faith it is impossible to please God, for the one who draws near to Him must believe that He exists and rewards those who seek Him.

Many years ago we had a tragedy in our church. Three people were slain, and we had a triple funeral; all three caskets lined up in front of the stage. It was a horrendous week, and by Sunday night I didn't have anything left in my heart to say. So when time came for the evening sermon, I simply opened to Hebrews 11 and read it, all forty verses. Then I closed my Bible, pronounced the benediction, and sent everyone home. I was surprised by the impact. People were deeply moved, openly weeping. One man who was sobbing as he left told me he'd never known such power was contained in this chapter.

The theme of the book of Hebrews is perseverance. It was written to a group of Jewish Christians who were encountering opposition, and the writer was worried that some would give up on the gospel. In chapter 10 he reminds them of previous days when they had been publicly exposed to taunts and afflictions (v. 33), and some had incurred the confiscation of their possessions (v. 34). He warns them not to throw away their confidence (v. 35) but to exercise endurance (v. 36).

That brings us to chapter 11, in which he holds up the great persevering heroes of the Old Testament. This is called the "Faith Chapter of the Bible," the "Westminster Abby of Scripture," and "Faith's Hall of Fame." The chapter begins by giving us the Bible's classic definition of faith, in verse 1: "Now faith is the reality of things hoped for, the proof of what is not seen." And according to verse 6, without this kind of faith, it's impossible to please God. Those who come to Him must believe He exists and that He rewards those who earnestly seek Him.

Here are four reasons faith is necessary for pleasing God.

1. *Faith brings salvation to our lives.* As we've seen in previous verses, we are saved by grace through faith.
2. *Faith brings motivation to our work.* The main theme of Hebrews 11 is that faith leads us to do things for God we would never otherwise do. It motivates, fuels, and drives our labor. The very next verse (v. 7) tells how Noah, by faith, built an ark to save his family.
3. *Faith brings rest to our souls.* When we're tempted to fret and fear, we discover that God has given us multiple promises and assurances for every contingency in life.
4. *Faith brings excitement to our future.* We look forward by faith to a city whose builder and maker is God (vv. 10, 16).

※ [Faith] glorifies God exceedingly, because it proves that we have more confidence in His eyesight than in our own.[127]—C. H. Mackintosh

SENT:

The Great Commission and Our Global Task

83. Matthew 28:18

> *Then Jesus came near and said to them, "All authority has been given to Me in heaven and on earth."*

Matthew's book, the most Jewish of the Gospels and the one immediately joined to the last page of the Old Testament, ends with Christ's Great Commission to the whole world. Matthew begins his account by designating Christ the son of David, son of Abraham, and King of the Jews (1:1; 2:2); and he ends it with a missionary mandate to the nations (28:18–20).

Furthermore, it's incredible that Matthew didn't choose to conclude his Gospel by describing our Lord's spectacular ascension. He doesn't even end with a promise of Christ's return. He says nothing about the coming of the Holy Spirit. The last chapter of the first Gospel climaxes and ends, abruptly and dramatically, with a command to take the news of Christ's resurrection to the last place on earth until the last day of history.

If you read chapter 28 carefully, you'll notice there are actually two other "great commissions" leading up to this final "Great Commission."

In verses 6–7, the angel told the women at the tomb: "He is not here! For He has been resurrected, just as He said. Come and see. . . . Then go quickly and tell."

In verse 10, Jesus Himself intercepted the women as they ran from the tomb. "Go and tell," He commanded them.

Then in verses 18–20, we're all commanded to "go and tell," and this command is preceded by an all-encompassing claim. Jesus declares that all authority is His in heaven and on earth. With that supreme authority, then, He has appointed you and me to do our bit, throughout every day and wherever we go, to spread His good news.

The Great Commission was apparently spoken by Christ on a mountainside in Galilee. We know the eleven apostles were there, but perhaps He had a larger audience. As far as we know, this is the only time the risen Christ made a prearranged appearance. The other ten or so postresurrection appearances were unannounced; but this one was arranged by Jesus in advance and explained to the disciples even before He died on the cross (Matt. 26:32; 28:7, 10, 16). There's no indication this was secret information so presumably the disciples came with their families, children, and friends in tow; and this is likely the time when a crowd of five hundred saw the risen Savior (1 Cor. 15:6). Some of these, having only heard the rumors of the resurrection, were doubtful (Matt. 28:17). Seeing Him in the distance, they questioned. But as He came closer, they all saw Him and worshipped (vv. 17–18). The words Jesus spoke have fueled the mission of the church for two thousand years and will propel its ministries until He returns.

※ The Great Commission is not an option to be considered; it is a command to be obeyed.—Hudson Taylor

84. Matthew 28:19

Go, therefore and make disciples of all nations, baptizing them in the name of the Father and of the Son and of the Holy Spirit.

The Great Commission is easy to memorize if you keep in mind its five great components.

1. **His power.** At our church we sometimes have a commissioning service for missionaries leaving to serve in other places. Matthew 28 gives us our Lord's commissioning service for every Christian. The Great Commission begins with Christ's assertion of authority over heaven and earth. He has the right to send us even to those who don't invite us to come. We're authorized to go with the full backing of His unlimited power and authority.

2. **His purpose.** We're to make disciples. Literally this passage says, "As you are going, make disciples." A disciple is someone who confesses Christ as Lord, is actively growing in His Word, and is fully committed to His purpose of making other disciples.

3. **His place.** Our zone of ministry is the world: "all nations." In Matthew 24, Jesus predicted the gospel would be preached in the whole world as a testimony to all nations before He returns.

4. **His plan**. Disciple-making involves two simple steps— baptizing and teaching. Baptizing implies we've shared the gospel and led someone to receive it. Then we must teach that person. Notice that Jesus doesn't say, "teaching them everything I have commanded you," but, "teaching them *to observe* everything I have commanded you." Discipleship isn't just a matter of book learning, but of lifestyle transformation.

5. **His presence**. Just as Jesus began His Commission by asserting His power, He ended by promising His presence.

He'll abide with us always, to the end of the age. He's a very present help, a Friend who sticks closer than a brother, and the unseen Partner in all our efforts for His kingdom.

Ever notice how God made every living thing to propagate? I can't get over how persistently the plants spread in my little garden. Stubborn weeds and grasses shoot across the mulch, creating entrenched aggravations for me. Nearby raspberries launch new stems like meteors, shooting through the air, landing, taking root, and sending out more stems to nearby spots. The neighboring maple trees send out an air force of helicopters that drop their seeds like bombs all over my vegetable beds and flowerpots. So it shouldn't come as a surprise that God built the same driving potential into His church. It is as natural for the church of Jesus Christ to spread as it is for weeds, raspberries, and maple trees. And, in fact, it's not just a potential and a pattern; it is a commandment. It is our commission. We're sent like human helicopters into this world to spread the message of Christ, person-to-person, until it covers the globe.

※ If a commission by an earthly king is considered an honor, how can a commission by a Heavenly King be considered a sacrifice? —David Livingstone

85. Matthew 28:20

Teaching them to observe everything I have commanded you. And remember, I am with you always, to the end of the age.

In memorizing this verse, I thought of missionary-explorer, David Livingstone, who leaned on it repeatedly during lonely treks through deepest Africa. Here's a sample from his journal on January 14, 1856, when threatened by hostile tribes.

I felt some turmoil of spirit in the evening at the prospect of having all my efforts for the welfare of this great region and its teeming population knocked on the head by savages tomorrow. . . . But I read that Jesus said, "All power is given unto Me in heaven and on earth; go ye, therefore, and teach all nations . . . and lo, I am with you always, even unto the end of the world." I took this as His word of honor, and then went out to take observations for latitude and longitude, which, I think, were very successful."[128]

The promise of God's presence is a potent reality for every Christian worker. It was originally given to the eleven disciples on a hillside in Galilee; and it so deeply impressed one of them—Matthew—that he chose to end His Gospel with these words rather than by recording our Lord's ascension into heaven or the promise of His return.

What a joy to practice constantly the presence of the Lord!

Missionary Rosalind Goforth told of a time when she and her family were in extreme danger during the Boxer Rebellion in China. They were surrounded by a bloodthirsty mob, and Rosalind was seized with overwhelming fear—not of dying but of being tortured, which was a likely scenario. Her husband drew from his pocket a little book of Bible verses and read, "The eternal God is thy refuge, and underneath are the everlasting arms" (Deut. 33:27). He went on to recite several similar verses.

"The effect of those words at such a time was remarkable," said Rosalind. "All realized that God was speaking to us. Never was there a message more directly given to mortal man from God than that message to us. From almost the first verse my whole soul seemed flooded with a great peace; all trace of panic vanished; and I felt God's presence was with us. Indeed, His presence was so real it scarcely (could) have been more so had we seen a visible form."[129] This promise isn't just for missionaries in dangerous times. The abiding presence of the Lord Jesus is a blessing to every child of God.

❉ But I return without misgiving and with great gladness. For would you like me to tell you what supported me through all the years of exile among people whose language I could not understand, and whose attitude toward me was often hostile? It was this: "Lo, I am with you always, even unto the end of the world." On those words I staked everything, and they never failed.—David Livingstone in an address at Glasgow University before returning to Africa

86. Acts 1:8

But you will receive power when the Holy Spirit
has come upon you, and you will be My witnesses in
Jerusalem, in all Judea and Samaria, and to the ends of
the earth.

Acts 1:8 is the key that unlocks the door of Acts and the gates of Christian history.

Acts 1:8 represents the last known words of Jesus during His earthly ministry. Verse 9 indicates these are the Lord's final words before being "taken up." Luke 24:50–53 says Jesus ascended to heaven while blessing His disciples, but His words of blessings aren't given. Acts 1:8 are His final words as they were recorded for us. Shouldn't His last command be our first concern?

Acts 1:8 represents the passing of the baton between the Son and the Spirit regarding the divine mission on earth. Jesus indicated in the upper room discourse (John 13–17) that in His physical body He would return to heaven. His presence here would be replaced, so to speak, by the Holy Spirit; and He told the disciples in Luke 24 to tarry in Jerusalem until the Spirit arrived. In Acts 2 we have this arrival, the unleashing of the Holy Spirit upon the church. The book of Acts (and all subsequent Christian history) is the story of what Jesus Christ is continuing to do (see v. 1) on earth through His Spirit working in His church.

Acts 1:8 provides the table of contents for the book of Acts. In reading through Acts, it becomes clear that chapters 1–7 describe the gospel's penetrating Jerusalem; chapters 8–12, Judea and Samaria; and chapters 13–18, the ends of the earth, exactly as outlined in Acts 1:8.

Acts 1:8 represents Christ's agenda for the duration of history till He returns. It's our personal mandate, and every day of our lives must be spent under its ambition and authority.

A. W. Tozer on Acts 1:8

"Ye shall receive power." By those words our Lord raised the expectation of His disciples and taught them to look forward to the coming of a supernatural potency into their natures from a source outside of themselves. It was to be something previously unknown to them, but suddenly to come upon them from another world. It was to be nothing less than God Himself entering into them with the purpose of ultimately reproducing His own likeness within them. . . . This power is to come upon powerless men as a gentle but resistless invasion from another world bringing a moral potency infinitely beyond anything that might be stirred up from within. This power is sufficient; no additional help is needed, no auxiliary source of spiritual energy.[130]

※ Power came upon the Church, such power as had never been released into human nature before (with the lone exception of that mighty anointing which came upon Christ by the waters of Jordan). That power, still active in the Church, has enabled her to exist for nearly twenty centuries.[131]—A. W. Tozer

THE TWENTY-THIRD PSALM:

The Lord Is My Shepherd

87. Psalm 23:1

The LORD is my shepherd; there is nothing I lack.

The Twenty-third Psalm has been a source of strength and comfort for three thousand years. It is the most beloved poem in history, the most memorized passage in the Bible, and the most vivid allegory ever written. Some years ago when I went through a difficult period and couldn't sleep for anxiety, I found rest at night by repeating this psalm in my mind. It had a calming power found nowhere else.

As a boy-shepherd, David saw that his relationship with his flock was like the Lord's relationship with him. He was utterly dependent on someone to care for him.

Unlike many animals, sheep can't make it on their own. They can't fight with their hoofs or teeth. They can't track down food. They can't run very easily, or dig holes, or climb trees to escape predators. They can't kick or bite. They need a shepherd to care for them, just as we do. That's why Psalm 23 doesn't say, "The Lord is *a* shepherd," or "The Lord is *the* shepherd." It says, "The Lord is *my* shepherd." And if He is my Shepherd, I will not lack.

- I shall not lack peace and provision, for He gives green pastures and still waters.
- I shall not lack hope and encouragement, for He restores my soul.
- I shall not lack guidance, for He leads me in paths of righteousness for His name's sake.
- I shall not lack deliverance in tough times, for He's with me even in the valley of shadows.
- I shall not lack protection, for His rod and staff comfort me, and He prepares a table for me in the presence of my enemies.
- I shall not lack help and healing in all the events of life, for He anoints my head with oil.
- I shall not lack endless blessings, for my cup overflows, and goodness and mercy will follow me all my days.
- I shall not lack eternal life and heaven, for I will dwell in the house of the Lord forever.

MEMORY TIP

If you've already memorized the Twenty-third Psalm, why not learn it in a singable version? One of the most famous British hymns is the Scottish version of Psalm 23, set to the tune "Crimond." The first stanza says: *The Lord's my Shepherd, I'll not want; He makes me down to lie / In pastures green; He leadeth me, the quiet waters by.* It's easy to find both the words and tune on the Internet; and it may become one of your favorite hymns, as it is mine.

✳ Three thousand years have passed away since David sung this sweet song, and yet it is as new and fresh as if it had come to us this morning.[132]—J. Wilber Chapman

88. Psalm 23:2

He lets me lie down in green pastures; He leads me beside
quiet waters.

Sheep eat standing up. We once had a small flock, and the only time I saw them eat lying down was when sick. Sheep eat on all fours, then find a shady spot to lie down and chew their cud. When the psalmist said, "He lets me lie down in green pastures," he meant, "I'm well satisfied. I've had plenty to eat. My needs have been met. Now I'm going to settle down in contentment."

What about the still waters? Sheep are frightened by rushing streams, for they wear heavy woolen coats that can become waterlogged and result in drowning. Our sheep wouldn't come near the water trough while I was filling it with the hose. The sound and sight of the splashing bothered them. But when the water was stilled, they'd come and drink all they wanted.

If we're under the Shepherd's ownership and care, He'll see to it that every need in our lives is met in one way or another—our external needs, our internal needs, and our eternal needs.

Our job is to graze in the sweet pasturage of the Word and to drink from the still waters of the Spirit. A writer of yesteryear, William Evans, observed: "It is generally recognized as being a very difficult thing to get God's people to thus lie down. They will do almost anything and everything else but that. They will run, walk, fight, sing, teach, preach, work, in a word do almost anything and everything except seek seasons of quiet and periods of retirement for secret communion with God and quiet soul nurture. . . . We do not like pauses . . . from the rush into the hush (to which) Jesus calls us."[133]

During some seasons of the year, our sheep drank little or nothing from their trough. We learned that if the climate is right, sheep can go for a long time without actually drinking water because of the heavy dews. When the grass is sopping wet, the sheep take in their needed moisture with their nutrition. It's a wonderful picture of the Spirit-drenched Scriptures. In the early morning we graze in the sweet pasturage of the Word of God covered with the watery dew of the Holy Spirit. What an apt image of the Christian's daily quiet time.

MEMORY TIP

Spare no effort to learn this psalm. The Twenty-third Psalm has been memorized by every generation from antiquity to modernity. It's been quoted across the centuries and through the millennia. In just six verses amounting to about a hundred words, it sums up all our needs in life and all the gracious provisions of God's grace. Learn it a verse at a time, and each verse will build on the preceding one. Remember: It begins in "green pastures" and ends "in the house of the Lord forever."

※ My faithful Shepherd is the Lord, supplying all my needs; In pastures green He makes me rest, by quiet waters leads.—The Presbyterian Psalter

89. Psalm 23:3

He renews my life; He leads me along the right paths for
His name's sake.

Many biblical heroes were shepherds. Abraham, Isaac, Jacob, and the patriarchs were shepherds. Moses was shepherding when God called him to deliver the Israelites. King David started life as a shepherd, and the lessons he learned prepared him for the kingship. It seems that leading sheep was good preparation for leading people. The prophet Amos was a shepherd whom the Lord took from tending his flocks to preaching to Israel. The announcement of the birth of Christ was made to shepherds keeping watch over their flocks by night. In the Old Testament Jehovah is described as our Shepherd; and in the New Testament Jesus said, "I am the good shepherd" (John 10:11).

If we want to understand God's Word and His ways, we have to know something about biblical shepherding. One of the most important things was leading the flock to the right place by the right route. As the summer heated up, lower pastures became barren, forcing the shepherd to lead his sheep to higher pastures. Sheep easily overgrazed an area, and that, too, created a need for new pasturelands. The shepherd had to know where those were located and how to get there. He couldn't afford to lead his flock into dead-end canyons or into areas with no water or that were off limits. He had to go before the flock, check out the pathway, locate available grazing lands, and lead his flock there in safety.

To biblical writers this was analogous to God's guidance. He restores our souls, giving us the dispositions we need; and He leads us in the right paths, giving us the directions He wants us to take.

Other Great "Guidance Verses" in the Bible:

- Proverbs 3:5–6: Trust in the LORD with all your heart, and do not rely on your own understanding; think about Him in all your ways, and He will guide you on the right paths.
- Psalm 37:23: A man's steps are established by the LORD, and He takes pleasure in his way.
- Psalm 139:16: All my days were written in Your book and planned before a single one of them began.
- Isaiah 48:17: I am the LORD your God, who teaches you for your benefit, who leads you in the way you should go.
- Psalm 32:8: I will instruct you and show you the way to go; with My eye on you, I will give counsel.
- Psalm 48:14: This God, our God forever and ever—He will lead us eternally.
- Psalm 73:24: You guide me with Your counsel, and afterwards You will take me up in glory.

※ Savior, like a shepherd lead us, much we need Thy tender care.
—Dorothy Thrupp

90. Psalm 23:4

*Even when I go through the darkest valley, I fear no
danger, for You are with me; Your rod and Your staff—
they comfort me.*

The key to understanding Psalm 23 is recognizing that it's geographically progressive. This was a flock on the move. It began in the
lowlands near Bethlehem, the Negev, or Jericho, where spring pastures
were available. As the summer progressed, the flocks migrated northward, eventually arriving in the tablelands referred to in the next verse
("You prepare a table before me"). In Genesis 37:14–17, the sons of Jacob
followed a similar itinerary with their flocks, going northward from
Hebron, to Shechem, to Dothan. This trekking inevitably led through
valleys and canyons.

Verse 4 begins with the words "even when," linking it to the preceding verse. God leads us in the right paths, even when our circumstances
appear dark and difficult. Sometimes our route threads through dark
valleys as we face stress and strain, grief and sadness. During such times
we "fear no danger, for You are with me; Your rod and Your staff—they
comfort me."

The shepherd's presence was the greatest comfort for the sheep. So
was his rod, a club used against predators. The staff was helpful in snag-
ging sheep that strayed too near precipices.

With this verse we've reached the halfway point in Psalm 23, a com-
forting thought. It means the valley doesn't last forever. In the next verses
we'll discover highland tables, overflowing cups, unfailing goodness and
mercy, and an eternal home.

Notice that a subtle pronoun shift occurs in this verse. Until
now, it's been "The Lord . . . *He* . . ." He lets me lie down in green
pastures. . . . He renews. . . . He leads. . . . Now, in the valley, it becomes
You: "You are with me; Your rod and staff—they comfort me." At this
point the Twenty-third Psalm becomes a prayer.

When David wrote Psalm 23:4, he may have based his imagery on the wadi Kelt, a deep canyon near Bethlehem. In the Middle East, the word *wadi* designates a deep ravine or dry valley, and the wadi Kelt is a rugged canyon that stretches from the Jerusalem-Bethlehem area to the Jericho-Jordan River area. For many years when I led trips to Israel, I'd request a bus driver willing to drive us through the wadi Kelt. Not all drivers will take this route because of its drastic cliffs and hairpin turns. On our last trip to the Holy Land, I was disappointed to learn that this old road was blocked by the Israeli government because suicide bombers were using the wadi Kelt to slip into Jerusalem from Jericho. We were only able to drive a portion of the way. This is the route Jesus would have taken in biblical times, and He used this location as the setting for His story about the good Samaritan. It's the traditional "valley of the shadow of death."

✻ The shadow of a dog cannot bite; the shadow of a sword cannot kill; the shadow of death cannot destroy us.—Charles Haddon Spurgeon

91. Psalm 23:5

You prepare a table before me in the presence of my ene-
mies; You anoint my head with oil; my cup overflows.

As the geography of Psalm 23 progresses, we have now reached the high plateaus and tablelands where the shepherd's muscles are put to the test. There are rocks to disgorge, briars to clear, pastures to cultivate for the flocks, water to be channeled, and mountain lions to be driven away. Our Shepherd provides for us even in remote places, even in the presence of predatory foes.

Sometimes we encounter human enemies, scheming coworkers, unpleasant neighbors, or hostile family members. Worse enemies lurk within us—selfish thoughts, filthy minds, jealous attitudes, or bitter spir-its. Most dangerous of all are satanic spiritual forces prowling around like roaring lions looking for sheep to devour.

Our Shepherd delivers us from all foes. Jesus said, "My sheep hear My voice, I know them, and they follow Me. I give them eternal life, and they will never perish—ever! No one will snatch them out of My hand" (John 10:27–28).

The Lord anoints us with oil of the Holy Spirit, soothing our hurts, nicks, cuts, bumps, and bruises. And as He tends to our needs, we can say, "Our cups run over!" Providing water for the sheep was hard work. In places without a natural source of water, wells were dug by hand with crude shovels. In Genesis 29, for example, Jacob came upon an enormous well in Mesopotamia that serviced three different herdsmen. At a certain time each day, the workers would roll a stone from the mouth of the well and haul up the water, pouring it into troughs till they overflowed. To the psalmist, such a scene illustrated God's overflowing blessings in our lives.

One day when I was checking on our sheep, I was alarmed to find that the horse had taken a bite out of the ear of one of our ewes. I didn't see it happen, but there was no doubt that a good portion of her ear had been torn away by the horse's teeth. At first I didn't know what to do, but I thought of this verse of Scripture. Grabbing a bottle of olive oil from the kitchen, I washed the damaged ear and rubbed that olive oil into the wound. It seemed to soothe the sheep, and after several treatments, the wound healed. Later as I was talking to a sheep farmer about it, he said, "Oh, yes, that's a little trick we use at livestock shows. If we're showing a sheep and she gets a nick or a cut, we rub a little olive oil on it, and it does the trick."

✳ There is no grudging in God's benevolence; He does not measure out His goodness as the apothecary counts his drops. . . . God's way is always characterized by . . . overflowing bounty.[134]—F. B. Meyer

92. Psalm 23:6

*Only goodness and faithful love will pursue me all the
days of my life, and I will dwell in the house of the LORD
as long as I live.*

The Twenty-third Psalm is a genius of simplicity, and this final verse
has two simple points: If the Lord is our Shepherd, we have goodness and
mercy *behind* us and our Father's House *before* us.

The word *goodness* in this verse means "benefits, desirable realities,
welfare, prosperity, happiness, blessings." It's an all-inclusive word that
implies we have a good God who does only good things and who gives
only good gifts to those who know Him.

The phrase *faithful love* or *mercy* is from a great Old Testament
word for the steadfast love of God, whose nature it is to be forgiving
and benevolent. He surrounds our lives with acts of kindness we don't
deserve, all because of His loyal and royal love for us.

The verb is *pursue.* The Hebrew term David originally used was a
proactive term, meaning "to chase." It's as if David were saying that these
two qualities—goodness and mercy—are like God's sheepdogs. Often
in sheepherding lands, you'll see a shepherd going in front of the flock,
followed by the sheep. Bringing up the rear and running along the sides
are the sheepdogs that help with the herding.

It's fascinating to read about herding dogs. They're found all over
the world in every kind of agricultural society. They're working animals,
trained to the sound of a whistle or a word, that keep the flock or herd
on the trail. They typically stay behind the flock, and they use their
barks and aggressive movements to keep the sheep moving in the desired
directions. Goodness and mercy are God's border collies, chasing us,
following us, guiding us, surrounding us on every side, all the days of
our lives.

And afterward? Afterward we will live with Him forever in His
home. Here Psalm 23 comes full circle. The shepherd has led his flock
into the green pastures of the spring meadows. As the summer progressed

and the pastures receded, he led them through mountain passes and deep valleys to higher ground. Now as winter approaches, he brings them back down the hillsides toward home, back to the folds prepared for them, being herded by goodness and mercy.

And there, in our Father's house, we will dwell with the Lord forever.

The King of Love my Shepherd is,
Whose goodness faileth never.
I nothing lack if I am His
And He is mine forever.

Where streams of living water flow,
My ransomed soul he leadeth,
And where the verdant pastures grow,
With food celestial feedeth.

Perverse and foolish oft I've strayed,
And yet in love He sought me,
And on His shoulders gently laid,
And home rejoice brought me.

And so through all the length of days
Thy goodness faileth never;
Good Shepherd, may I sing Thy praise,
Within Thy house forever.
—Henry Baker

※ The totality of His grace for the totality of our lives for the duration of eternity—that's Psalm 23:6.—Anonymous

ALPHA AND OMEGA:

The First and Second Comings of Christ

93. Isaiah 9:6

> *For a child will be born for us, a son will be given to us,*
> *and the government will be on His shoulders. He will*
> *be named Wonderful Counselor, Mighty God, Eternal*
> *Father, Prince of Peace.*

Written seven hundred years before Christ, this verse caps a remarkable passage of prophecy about the Messiah to come. Isaiah 9 predicts He will headquarter in Galilee (v. 1), will be a light that dispels gloom and a liberator who brings joy (vv. 1–5), will come as a child born, as a son given. He'll permanently occupy the throne of David, and there will be no end to His rule (v. 7). We're then given a set of majestic titles that describe His role. He will be:

The Wonderful Counselor. We sometimes need a financial counselor, a legal counselor, a career counselor, or perhaps a marriage counselor. Jesus is the *Wonderful* Counselor, and we can study the Gospels to see how unfailingly He counseled all who came to Him. As He prepared to return to heaven, He told His disciples, "I will ask the Father, and He will give you another Counselor to be with you . . . the Holy Spirit" (John 14:16, 26).

The Mighty God. In the Bible divine characteristics were assigned to Him, divine works credited to Him, divine worship rendered to Him, and divine titles ascribed to Him. He is both God and man.

The Everlasting Father. This doesn't mean that Jesus is the first person of the Trinity. Jesus is God, but He isn't the Father or the Holy Spirit. He's the second person of the Trinity; and from everlasting to everlasting, He exercises fatherly care over us as One who perfectly represents the Father's love for us.

The Prince of Peace. He possesses infinite peace, which He imparts to His own. In Him we have peace with God, peace throughout life, peace at the moment of death, and everlasting peace in heaven. These four titles are given so we can know Him better, worship Him fully, and enjoy Him as our Counselor, God, Father, and Prince.

God the Son is called the Prince of Peace. He came into the world with a song of peace: "On earth peace. . . ." He went out of the world with a legacy of peace: "Peace I leave with you, My peace I give unto you." Christ's earnest prayer was for peace; He prayed that His people might be one. Christ not only prayed for peace, but bled for peace: "Having made peace through the blood of His cross." He died not only to make peace between God and man, but between man and man. Christ suffered on the cross, that He might cement Christians together with His blood; as He prayed for peace, so He paid for peace.[135]—Thomas Watson, seventeenth-century Puritan

---

※ Hail the heav'n born Prince of Peace! Hail the Son of righteousness! Light and life to all He brings, ris'n with healing in His wings.—Charles Wesley

94. Luke 2:10

*But the angel said to them, "Don't be afraid, for look,
I proclaim to you good news of great joy that will be for
all the people.*

Luke 2:10–12 is the Bible's classic Christmas text, sung by angels choiring over Shepherds' Field in Bethlehem: Don't be afraid, for look, I proclaim to you good news of great joy that will be for all the people: today a Savior, who is Messiah the Lord, was born for you in the city of David. This will be the sign for you: you will find a baby wrapped snugly in cloth and lying in a manger.[136] Never was so great a message delivered in so few words. Notice how the message unrolls as you read the text.

1. **This is liberating news.** *Don't be afraid.* The coming of Christ banishes fear from human hearts.
2. **This is supernatural news.** It was given by an angel from heaven shouting, *Look! I proclaim. . .*
3. **This is personal news.** *I proclaim to you. . . .*
4. **This is good news.** *I proclaim to you good news. . . .*
5. **This is happy news.** *I proclaim to you good news of great joy. . . .*
6. **This is global news.** *. . . that will be for all the people.*
7. **This is breaking news.** *Today . . .*
8. **This is saving news.** *Today a Savior . . .*
9. **This is Messianic news.** *Today a Savior, who is Messiah. . . .*
10. **This is divine news.** *Today a Savior, who is Messiah the Lord.*
11. **This is baby news.** *Today a Savior, who is Messiah the Lord, was born for you. . . .*
12. **This is royal news.** *. . . born for you in the city of David.*
13. **This is accessible news.** *This will be the sign for you: you will find a baby wrapped snugly in cloth and lying in a manger.*

From time to time I've had the joy of leading tours to the Holy Land, and one of my favorite spots is Shepherds' Field outside Bethlehem. Since Bethlehem was encircled by fields on every side, we don't know the exact location of the events of Luke 2; but the traditional spot is a rock-strewn field that's rather bowl shaped, with sloping sides all around. The upper rim is dotted with ancient caves, where, according to tradition, the shepherds slept in shifts during the long, cold nights. It's not hard to imagine caroling angels hovering over this field. Their message was a universal announcement to all history yet so very personal: *I proclaim to you . . . was born for you . . . you will find a baby. . . .* It was for you . . . you . . . you . . . that He came, and for me. His name, Emmanuel, means "God with us."

※ We cannot approach the manger of the Christ child in the same way we approach the cradle of another child. Rather, when we go to His manger, something happens, and we cannot leave it again unless we have been judged or redeemed.[137]—Dietrich Bonhoeffer

95. Luke 2:11

*Today a Savior, who is Messiah the Lord, was born for
you in the city of David.*

The world was perfectly aligned for the first advent of our Lord
Jesus; He was born in the fullness of time. Messiah arrived when the
nation of Israel was a viable province in the political world, anchored by
its capital, Jerusalem. Jews of the Dispersion were scattered everywhere,
providing footholds for the preaching of the early evangelists. The Pax
Romana gave stability to the world, and the Roman roads contributed
to the spread of the gospel. The Greek language was universally spoken,
which aided the rapid spread of Christianity.

Now world events are aligning for His second advent. Every day the
headlines warn of our brittle economy, the globalization of commerce,
the secularization of culture, the nuclearization of the Middle East, the
threat of global pandemics, the persecution of Christians, the rise of
Islam, and the continued spread of the gospel. World leaders talk of a new
world order, and openly discuss a one-world currency. On every side are
wars and rumors of war, false prophets, famines, and earthquakes.

The Bible says when we see these things aligning in these ways, we
should lift our heads, for our redemption draws near. The message of
Christmas isn't for one day a year. Every day is a celebration that Jesus
has come, every day an anticipation of His return.

When Jesus came the first time, He came wrapped in swaddling clothes. When He comes again, He'll be dressed in the vestments of victory.

When He came the first time, there was no room in the inn. When He comes again, the whole world will be His domain.

He came the first time as King of the Jews. He will come again as King of kings and Lord of lords.

He came the first time to be crucified. He will come again to be glorified.

He came the first time as the Author of our salvation. He will come again as the Finisher of our faith.

He came the first time with a baby's cry. When He comes again, it will be with the roar of the lion of the tribe of Judah.

His first coming was known only to a few shepherds, a handful of wise men, and a few residents of Bethlehem. When He comes again, it'll be as lightning flashing east to west, He will come in the clouds of glory, and the entire universe will hear the news.

When He came at Bethlehem, the angels sang, "Glory to God in the highest" (Luke 2:15 NKJV). When He comes again, they will sing, "The kingdoms of this world have become the kingdoms of our Lord and of His Christ, and He shall reign forever and ever" (Rev. 11:15 NKJV).[138]

※ If we prepare well for Christmas, and keep Christmas well when it comes, I think we shall prepare well and be ready to meet Jesus Christ when he comes again.[139]—Edward Osborne

96. Luke 2:12

This will be the sign for you: you will find a baby
wrapped snugly in cloth and lying in a manger.

The angels called it a sign: "This will be a sign for you." In other words, they were telling the shepherds how to recognize the Savior. He'd be wrapped tightly in swaddling clothes, lying in a manger—probably in a cave. The likelihood of finding any baby lying in an animal's feeding bin was remote. So finding Him just as the angels described Him would be an indication their message was true in its totality.

According to the book *The New Manners and Customs of the Bible*, the clothes in which Jesus was wrapped were commonly referred to as swaddling clothes because they were like bandages, tightly wrapped around a newborn child to hold his legs and arms still. This is still widely practiced in some countries, as I've seen myself on overseas trips. In some cultures infants are wrapped up papoose-style. I used to think it cruel until I recalled that a newborn infant was pretty tightly contained in the womb, too.

But there's something more here.

It's impossible to think of these words of Luke 2:12 without remembering the burial of Christ, when He was again tightly swathed in white reams of cloth and laid to rest in a cave under the watchful eyes of angels. The parallels between His birth and His burial are remarkable. Swaddled in white strips. In a cave. Resting. Redemptive. His mother watching. Angels hovering near.

And He didn't stay in either cave very long.

Bethlehem and Jerusalem are only about five miles apart, and the events were separated by only thirty-three years. But what mystery! Who can comprehend the Almighty lying in a manger, or the God of glory in a tomb? As Martin Luther said, "No other God have I but Thee; born in a manger, died on a tree."

Add verses 13 and 14 to your memory work, and you'll forever know the entire angelic carol, as recorded in the Gospel of Luke: Suddenly there was a multitude of the heavenly host with the angel, praising God and saying: "Glory to God in the highest heaven, and peace on earth to people He favors!"

Luke's Gospel was written in Greek; but in the mid-300s, verse 14 was translated in Latin by St. Hilary of Poitiers, and the phrase Hilary created has become famous:

Gloria, in excelsis Deo!

It became a widely used doxology in the Eastern Church where early Byzantine monks reportedly used it as an exclamation of praise not just at Christmas but every morning. And why not? Every day we should say, "This is the day the LORD has made!" Every morning we can truly proclaim, Gloria, in excelsis Deo! Glory to God in the highest!

❋ He looked into our globe and saw our grief; we look into His manger and see His answer.—Rob Morgan

97. Acts 1:11

They said, "Men of Galilee, why do you stand looking
up into heaven? This Jesus, who has been taken from you
into heaven, will come in the same way that you have
seen Him going into heaven."

Jesus entered and exited the world dramatically. He emerged from
the womb of a virgin, and He disappeared by slipping into the clouds. As
the disciples were peering into heaven at our Lord's ascension, two angels
addressed them with this memory verse. To my mind the most interesting words are "in the same way," indicating there are definite parallels
between His ascension and His return.

1. **His return will be literal.** This same Jesus will return,
    physically and bodily; Jesus said, "A ghost does not have flesh
    and bones as you see I have" (Luke 24:39).
2. **His return will be visible.** Jesus was "taken up as they were
    watching." Many passages tell us the second coming will be a
    visible event (Zech. 12:10; Rev. 1:7; Mark 14:62; Matt. 24:30).
3. **His return will be in the clouds.** The Bible makes a point
    of telling us that Jesus will come again in clouds of glory.
    Just as a cloud received Him at His ascension, the clouds will
    accompany His return (Dan. 7:13; Matt. 24:30; 26:64;
    1 Thess. 4:16; and Rev. 1:7). That's the reason God gives
    us so many beautiful skyscapes.
4. **His return will be to the Mount of Olives.** He ascended
    from here, and according to Zechariah 14:4, here He will
    return.

Our son-in-law, Ethan, was gone for many months during his military training. Everyone missed him, of course, especially Lily, age one. Victoria kept Ethan's picture nearby and told her he was coming back some day. Last Friday night Katrina and I put Lily in her crib about 8:30. A half hour later Victoria drove in from Fort Lee with Ethan. We sat and talked a few minutes, then Victoria went to the crib, gently lifted Lily out, and sat on the sofa beside Ethan. The little girl, still mostly asleep, opened her eyes and saw her dad. For a couple of minutes she gazed at him; you could see wheels turning in her mind. Then she grinned. She looked away, but her eyes darted back, and the two of them smiled and played eye games. Lily reached out and touched Ethan lightly, then started slapping at him. Next she leaned over and squirmed against him. All at once she was in his arms, kissing him with her open-mouthed wet kisses and hugging him, and she hasn't let go since.

I can't help wondering if that's a little picture of how we'll feel when we see Jesus.

※ He shall so come in like manner. . . . By any fair interpretation this can mean nothing short of a visible and bodily coming. It may mean more than that. It cannot mean less.[140]—R. A. Torrey

98. Revelation 21:1

*Then I saw a new heaven and a new earth, for the first
heaven and the first earth had passed away, and the sea
existed no longer.*

The final two chapters of the Bible are a virtual travel brochure of
heaven. If you're like me, you love travel guidebooks and brochures. My
bedside table is stacked with books about places I'd like to visit and trips
I'd like to make. At the top of the list is Revelation 21–22, the ultimate
travel guide. It's a description of heaven.

Too many of us have a vaporous view of eternity. We picture it as
clouds, harps, robes, and never-ending worship services. But the Bible
teaches that God is going to recreate the universe and give us a new
planet Earth. This new Earth will be a lot like the old one, only imperishable. No sin or sinners. No sorrow or suffering. No pain or pollution.
No tears. No death.

"Earth" is not a nebulous word. It's a real place with rivers, trees,
fields, and cities; the new Earth will be undoubtedly similar, only without the vast oceanic wastelands. Often when I'm visiting a beautiful place
like Yosemite National Park, I think of the words of an old song that says,
"How beautiful heaven must be." Those who know Christ will enjoy the
beauties of the new heaven, the new Earth, and the new city of Jerusalem
forever. What anticipation!

Anticipation is the most positive of positive emotions.
As children, we grow excited over upcoming events like
Christmas morning, birthdays, and trips to Disneyland. As we
age, we mustn't lose that wondering sense of anticipation.
I still look forward enormously to my trips, reading everything
I can about the place I'm planning to see. The anticipation is
as enjoyable as the actual event.

I read about one study in which volunteers were told they had won a free dinner at a fabulous French restaurant and were asked when they would like to eat there. Now? Tonight? Tomorrow? The meal was available at any time, but most of volunteers put off the dinner for a week or so. Researchers discovered that in doing so, the participants not only enjoyed the meal, but they had a full seven days of looking forward to it. As one man put it, "Forestalling pleasure is an inventive technique for getting double the juice from half the fruit."[141]

The dictionary defines *anticipation* as "pleasurable expectation." The Bible calls it hope. It is certainty centered not probability based, and our ultimate and greatest hope is eternal life in the new heaven, the new Earth, and the new city.

※ The first earth serves as the prototype or pattern for the new earth. There's continuity between old and new. We should expect new trees, new flowers, new rocks, new rivers, new mountains, and new animals. As our current bodies are the blueprints for our resurrection bodies, this present earth is the blueprint for the new earth.[142]—Randy Alcorn

99. Revelation 21:2

*I also saw the Holy City, new Jerusalem, coming down
out of heaven from God, prepared like a bride adorned
for her husband.*

At the dawning of eternity, the Lord will undertake the most massive relocation project in history. He will move an entire city out of the highest heaven, and it will descend to this Earth like a bride walking down the aisle for her groom. That's the picture the Lord uses to help us visualize this great, shimmering city, which will descend on beams of light and settle down on its perfectly designed foundation on the eternal Earth. As it does so, a herald will make the great announcement in verses 3–4: "Look! God's dwelling is with men, and He will live with them. . . . He will wipe away every tear from their eyes."

Revelation 21–22 takes us on a tour of this celestial city of Foreveropolis.

1. **The city from a distance** (Rev. 21:9–11). Standing atop a mountain, John watched this massive diamond of a city descend to the new Earth.

2. **The city up close** (vv. 12–14). As it grew nearer, he marveled at the massive walls, foundations, and gates.

3. **The size of the city** (vv. 15–17). Fourteen hundred miles in all directions!

4. **The construction of the city** (vv. 18–21). The building materials included gold, jewels, pearls, and crystal.

5. **The interior of the city** (vv. 22–23). John was impressed by the light illumining the city and by the absence of a temple.

6. **The commerce of the city** (vv. 24–27). Its gates are never shut as the produce and commodities of the new Earth flow in and out of it.

7. **The city center** (vv. 22:1–2). At the heart of the city are the throne, the Crystal River, the Golden Boulevard, and Tree of Life Park.

8. **The city's inhabitants** (vv. 3–5). God's children will be there worshipping, serving, reigning, and ruling forever with Him.

Looking for a City

- There is a river—its streams delight the city of God. (Ps. 46:4)
- I am going away to prepare a place for you. (John 14:2)
- [Abraham] was looking forward to the city that has foundations, whose architect and builder is God. (Heb. 11:10)
- God is not ashamed to be called their God, for He has prepared a city for them. (Heb. 11:16)
- You have come to . . . the city of the living God (the heavenly Jerusalem). (Heb. 12:22)
- For here we do not have an enduring city; instead, we seek the one to come. (Heb. 13:14)
- The city was pure gold like clear glass. (Rev. 21:18)

❋ As John watches . . . , an entire city, magnificent in its glory, descends whole from heaven and becomes part of the new earth. Heaven and earth are now one. The heavenly realm has moved its capital city to the new earth.[143]—John MacArthur

100. Revelation 22:20

He who testifies about these things says, "Yes, I am com-
ing quickly." Amen! Come, Lord Jesus!

This is the last promise and the final prayer in the Bible. It's also
the last of the "red letters" in the New Testament, bringing to an end
the actual spoken words of Christ in Scripture. Jesus is the one "who testifies about these things" and who promises, "Yes, I am coming quickly."
The word *testifies* is used in the sense of *declaring* or *proclaiming*; and
the phrase "these things" encompasses the entire book of Revelation. The
word *quickly* could mean either "suddenly" or "soon"—or both.

Three times in this chapter Jesus tells us He is coming quickly—in
verses 7, 12, and 20. It's a thrice-braided cord: *Look, I am coming quickly!*
Blessed is the one who keeps the prophetic words of this book. . . . Look! I am
coming quickly, and My reward is with Me. . . . Yes, I am coming quickly.

The immediate response of John in verse 20 was: "Amen!" This is
a term of agreement, meaning "so be it!" Then John offered the Bible's
concluding prayer: "Come, Lord Jesus!" This is the equivalent of the
Aramaic term *Maranatha*. It's a prayer for us to repeat frequently. What
a tragedy that Christians seldom pray specifically for the Lord to return.
Let's start including *Maranatha* in our prayer vocabulary.

Think of the excitement of knowing that Jesus is returning at any
moment!

In the darkest days of the Reformation in Scotland, when the hearts
of the faithful were low and languishing, John Knox accepted the invitation to return to his native land. Leaving Geneva, he bravely made
his way back to Scotland. According to A. J. Gordon's book *Ecce Venit*,
when Knox landed, word flashed across Scotland like lightning: "Knox
is back." Travelers suddenly mounted and sped into the country with the
tidings, "John Knox has come." At every cottage door the residents stood
and clustered, wondering, as horseman after horseman cried, "Knox has
come." Ships departing from the harbor bore up to each other at sea to
tell the news. Shepherds heard the tidings as they watched their flocks

upon the hills. The whole land was moved; the whole country was stirred with a new inspiration, and the hearts of the enemies withered."[144]

If the coming of a mere man could so electrify a nation, think of how we'll feel when our Lord appears in the clouds at any moment and calls us Home.

Maranatha! Even so, come, Lord Jesus!

Revelation 22

- The Bible's Last Beatitude (v. 14)
- The Last Invitation (v. 17)
- The Last Warning (v. 18–19)
- The Last Words of Jesus (v. 20)
- The Last Promise (v. 20)
- The Last Prayer (v. 20)
- The Last Benediction (v. 21)
- The Last Word: Amen (v. 21)

※ The promise (in this verse) is the culmination of all promises; and the response is the sum of all living hopes.[145]—The New Bible Commentary

More Life-Changing Verses I'm Committing to Memory

_____

_____

_____

_____

_____

_____

_____

_____

_____

Appendix: How to Memorize

—William Evans

Years ago Ruth Bell Graham, citing advice from C. S. Lewis, told me I should be a reader of old books. "For every new book you read," she said as I recall, "you should read an old one. The old books are best. People had time to think about what they were writing back then." A good place to start is with the prolific author, William Evans, an English-born Bible teacher who was connected with the Moody Bible Institute of Chicago and the Bible Institute of Los Angeles (BIOLA). His ministry spanned the first half of the twentieth century, and he was renowned for his Bible conference ministry. I'm indebted to my friend Lee Cope of Jackson, Mississippi, for giving me a copy of Evans's classic book about Scripture memory, *How to Memorize,* published by The Bible Institute Colportage Association of Chicago in 1909. Since it has long been out of print, I'm including this condensation as an appendix to my own book.

Chapter 1: The Importance of Having a Good Memory

Of what profit is all our wisdom, reading, and study if we are unable to preserve the knowledge we've acquired? Memory enriches the mind by preserving the results of our study and learning. It's the basis of all knowledge and the treasure of the mind.

Chapter 2: The Need of Cultivating the Memory

The inability to recall a thought or passage when needed has been a source of discomfort to many students. How often, on the other hand, has the ability to recall the desired passage been a means of strength in argument and a lifting up to a high place of worth in the estimation of those with whom we deal and among whom we work.

The other day a letter came from a minister in Michigan speaking of the value of knowing the Scriptures by heart. An infidel in his town had been able to argue successfully with all the ministers in the place. He gloried in the fact that he had beaten the ministers in their own arguments and that they had failed to convince him of the truth of the Bible. At last, however, he met his equal. It was a young student who knew much of the Bible by heart and had been taught the value of memory training. Said the infidel, "That young fellow seems to know every page in the Bible. He quoted Scripture to meet every objection I made. I am now convinced I was wrong, and I believe what I before doubted. Further, I am going to have this young man teach me more about the Bible."

Jesus broke the lance of the tempter by saying, "It is written . . ." He confounded His enemies more completely by His ready use of their own Scriptures than by His amazing miracles.

Chapter 3: The Possibilities of the Memory

The memory can be trained. There is no need of constantly forgetting. It's possible to acquire knowledge, learn names, and identify faces in such a way as to be able to recall them at pleasure. How pleased people are when we remember them. There is no need of forgetting what we have learned, providing we have learned it in the right way. There is no limit to the capacity of the memory. No one has ever learned so much that he cannot learn more. History furnishes wonderful accounts of memory achievements. Muretus, the French teacher of the sixteenth century, states he had a pupil, a young Corsican, who could repeat forward and backward thirty-six thousand unconnected words after hearing them but once. It was said of Dr. Johnson that he never forgot anything he had seen, heard, or read. Cyrus is said to have known the name of every soldier in his army. Tertullian, the great church father, devoted days and nights to memorizing the Scriptures, and got much of them by heart so accurately that he knew their very punctuation. To show the possibilities of memory training in old age, I refer to a New York editor who stated how, at age seventy-four, he began in a systematic way to commit Scriptures to memory. In a short time he was able to repeat a considerable part of the New Testament. Age is no barrier to success in memory training.

Chapter 4: What Is Memory?

Memory is our natural power of retaining what we learn and of recalling it on every occasion. It is a distinct faculty of the mind, different from perception, judgment, and reason. A good memory has three qualities: (1) the power to receive with comparative ease the words and phrases to be learned; (2) the power to store and retain them in the mind for an indefinite length of time; and (3) the reliableness to recall upon every proper occasion the words learned. Bad memories and weak memories can be overcome by strengthening and training.

Chapter 5: Preliminary Suggestions for the Training of the Memory

1. Each suggestion must be followed to the letter.
2. There should be *daily* practice to ensure the greatest possible amount of benefit. Set aside, if possible, the same hour each day in the same place. The morning is the best.
3. Be content, at first, with the mastery of *a little* each day. Many people fail in memory work by trying to accomplish too much at one sitting. Word upon word, line upon line, precept upon precept—let this be your rule.
4. Take *pleasure* in your study. Make yourself believe you like it whether you do or not. We learn easiest what we enjoy. Delight yourself, therefore, in your work, and great results can be expected.

5. Learn your lesson with the intention of remembering it *forever.* Many students learn a lesson merely for the recitation in class or for examination. Never cram for an occasion, but learn forever.

6. Remember that the aim is not the accumulation of a mass of memorized material, but to build up, strengthen, and train the memory to do its appointed work.

7. Be sure not to take up a second verse until you have *thoroughly mastered* the first.

Chapter 6: Attention, or Fixity of Thought

A poor memory has its origin in inattention. The secret of a good memory is our interest in and attention to a subject, as we rarely forget what has strongly impressed our minds. *Attention* is the directing of the mental powers to a specific object to the exclusion of all other objects. It means the setting of the mind upon a certain definite task. It is the power of mental concentration. The ability to fix our thought on what we desire to memorize is the first essential principle in the training of a good memory. To pin the thought, to fasten the attention on, and to allow no mind-wandering from the subject, to determine that the mind shall stretch itself over the subject under consideration in such a way as to shut out every intruding thought—this is to make memorizing possible, interesting, and delightful. A good memory is not to be expected until this power of attention is attained. If your mind wanders, bring it back again, and again, and yet again. Train your mind to read without wandering. Practice reading long passages of Milton, Shakespeare, or Emerson without letting your thoughts wander. The human mind is a great tramp; cure it of its vagrancy by keeping it at home. History tells us that so great was the power of concentration possessed by a writer in the time of the French Revolution that, although people were being massacred right under the window of the room in which he was engaged in writing a book, yet so absorbed was he in his subject that he knew nothing of what was happening on the outside until told afterward.

Chapter 7: A Clear Conception of the Matter to Be Memorized

You must have a clear conception of the matter you desire to memorize. Nothing less than a clear grasp and a definite understanding of the matter will suffice. Be sure you grasp it. It's a grievous mistake to think *words* are the only things to be memorized. We must obtain a clear conception of the thought contained in the words. Convert the text to a word picture and develop a visual memory. For example, in memorizing Psalm 15 we should read it over thoughtfully, noting the theme of the psalm, which is the person deemed worthy to abide in the temple of God. Form a mental picture of this person—what he is, what he does, what he does not do. Let your mental eye meet him. Listen to how he speaks. Having studied the passage and formed this mental picture, you may then proceed to take up the words of the psalm and memorize them. This you will now find to be a comparatively easy task. Most of the psalm has been learned in the very act of word-picturing. This pictorial faculty is essential to a good memory. It's also vital to read the passage aloud. Go into the open air, into the woods, or into the fields, and repeat it. Each repetition strengthens the impression made upon the memory. As a rule, do not memorize silently. If you do not have privacy, manipulate the lips and control the breath so as to whisper; but memorize with the mouth.

Chapter 8: Analyzing What You Desire to Memorize

It is a mistake to seek to memorize anything that has not been analyzed. To simply repeat the matter to be learned over and over again without any reference to the analysis of it is practically a waste of time so far as effective memory work is concerned. The best way to proceed is to arrange the matter to be learned analytically and synthetically. Take it to pieces and put it together again. By this process you will have almost learned the selection with scarcely any noticeable effort at memorizing. To memorize John 3:16, for example, find the shortest clause in the verse: *God loved*. Write that down. Write it again adding the next logical word. Write it again with the next logical work, and add one word after another until you have analyzed the whole verse. By then you will probably have practically memorized it. Be sure to write the words; it is not enough merely to repeat them aloud. Write them. WRITE. **WRITE.**

Chapter 9: Suggestive Association

Whatever has been perceived or conceived in connection with some other object or thought is afterwards suggestive of the other. Suggestive association is the connecting of a thought that is remote or abstract with others more obvious and familiar. In memorizing new matter, therefore, you must link it with a thought already in mind. Develop and use mnemonics. Psalm 37 and 73, for example, are simply reversed numerals, and both psalms deal with the question of the prosperity of the wicked. Matthew 20:28 and Acts 20:28 have the same numerical reference and both talk about being ransomed or purchased by the blood of Christ.

Chapter 10: The Power to Recall from Memory What You Have Learned

Recalling is different from reviewing. Recalling is an act of pure memory; reviewing, by the use of the text. Recalling must be absolutely from memory alone. Review during your study time, but seek to recall frequently.

Chapter 11: The Constant Practice of Reviewing

The lapse of time weakens the memory. Review daily. Suppose you determine to learn three verses a day. Having carried out your determination, review your newly acquired possession the same day. With each new daily lesson don't forget to review the lesson of the previous day and days. Continue this for a month, then spend a day reviewing. After three months spend a week reviewing. As you make more progress, judge for yourself how much time you need for review. To review, make cards of uniform size. On one side write the reference. On the other, write the text in full. Review first from one side then from the other so you learn both reference and verse. If, after having accumulated so many passages, you find it impossible to review every card, pick out a card here and there at random and review it. As you review a particular verse, note any cross-references that you can memorize and associate with that verse. You can learn the general contents of entire books by giving one- or two-word word titles to each chapter, using word associations, then mastering the list.

NOTES

1. James Allen, *As a Man Thinketh* (New York: Barnes & Noble Books, 2002), 22.

2. Ibid., 11.

3. Personal interview with Dr. Dallas Willard, used with permission. Willard's quotes are excerpted from a longer interview that appeared in my book, *Nelson's Annual Preacher's Sourcebook: 2008* (Nashville: Thomas Nelson, 2007), 59–61.

4. Based on phone conversations with Philip Turner and used with his permission.

5. Martin E. P. Seligman, *Learned Optimism* (New York: Alfred A. Knopf, 1991), 74–75.

6. Howard and Phyllis Rutledge with Mel and Lyla White, *In the Presence of Mine Enemies* (Old Tappan, NJ: Fleming H. Revell, 1973), excerpts taken from chapter 5.

7. On your next trip to Europe, don't look for the gardens of Hans Hugenberg; this is a fictional account I wrote as a description of the work the Master Gardener wants to do in our own minds.

8. Francis Cosgrove, "The Value of Scripture Memory," *Discipleship Journal,* Issue 9 (1982), 39.

9. Billy Graham, *How to Be Born Again* (Waco, TX: Word Books, 1977), 44–45.

10. Quoted in *The Biblical Expositor,* ed. Carl F. H. Henry (Philadelphia: A. J. Holman Company, 1960, 1973), xxiv.

11. Dan Martin, "Pastor, Wife Share Story of Their Daughter's Murder," *Baptist Press*, (October 15, 1998), 4.

12. Darlene Deibler Rose, *Evidence Not Seen: One Woman's Faith in a Japanese P.O.W. Camp* (Carlisle, UK: O. M. Publishing, 1988), 129–30.

13. L. Anderson, J. W. Hayford, and B. Patterson, *Who's in Charge? Standing Up to Leadership Pressures* (Sisters, OR: Multnomah Books, 1993), chapter 3.

14. John Crawford, "An Anchor for Your Heart," in *Discipleship Journal,* Issue 9 (1982), 40.

264 100 BIBLE VERSES EVERYONE SHOULD KNOW BY HEART

15. Based on conversations with BettyRuth Barrows Seera. I also relate this story in my book, *The Promise* (Nashville: B&H Publishing Group, 2008), 112–13.

16. The story about Samuel Wesley Jr. is found in Allan Longworth, *Samuel Wesley Junior* (Orangeburg, SC: Foundery Press, 1991), 3–4. The hymn can be located at various online hymn Web sites.

17. Quoted in *The Hand of God: Thoughts and Images Reflecting the Spirit of the Universe*, ed. Michael Reagan (Philadelphia and London: Templeton Foundation Press, 1999), 158.

18. J. B. T. Marsh, *Story of the Jubilee Singers, with Their Songs* (New York: S. W. Green's Sons, 1883), 109–10.

19. J. I. Packer, *Knowing God* (Downers Grove, IL: Intervarsity Press, 1973), 46.

20. Ibid., 47–48.

21. Samuel D. Gordon, *Quiet Talks about Jesus* (New York: A. C. Armstrong & Son, 1906), 13.

22. John 3:16 is the Bible in miniature and the gospel in a nutshell. But many of us who memorized John 3:16 in the older versions struggled with the phrase "only begotten Son." It often came out "only forgotten Son," to the amusement of our parents. Modern translations say, "His one-and-only Son." Why the change?

The Greek word is *monogenas* (mon'-o-ga-nase'). The prefix *mono* means "one" or "only." The word *genas* means "race, stock, family, class, kind, or of the same nature." *Monogenas* really means "the only one of its kind." When the New Testament began to be translated into Latin in ancient times, the first versions rendered used the Latin word *unicus*, meaning "unique." It was understood that the word *monogenas* was the Greek equivalent of the Latin word *unicus* and, by extension, of the English word *unique*. But the great scholar, Jerome, made a critical change. Perhaps he was influenced by the theological debates of his day, or perhaps he didn't fully understand the meaning of the Greek word. For whatever reason, when he created his famous Latin translation, the Vulgate, he didn't use the term that had been used by earlier Latin translators, *unicus*. He used the word *unigenitus*, which meant "only begotten."

Jerome's translation became the standard Bible for a thousand years, and it led to many of the early English versions, including the King James Version. Today's scholars widely agree that the word *monogenes* means "unique, one of a kind, one and only." Jesus is utterly unique in human history and in the chronicles of time. He existed before the world began yet was born under Judean skies in the days of Herod the Great. He is in very nature God, yet He slipped into humanity like a hand into a glove. He is the Son of the Highest yet the Son of a Jewish virgin. He is worshipped of angels yet was crucified with thieves. He was vilified by the world but deified by the Father. He is morally perfect, yet He became sin for us. He is a Man of sorrows, yet He manufactures joy for the universe. He is the ultimate demonstration of love, for God loved the world enough to give His one and only Son, that everyone who believes in Him will not perish but have everlasting life.

23. V. Raymond Edman, *But God* (Grand Rapids: Zondervan, 1962), 102.

24. Bill Hybels and Mark Mittelberg, *Becoming a Contagious Christian* (Grand Rapids: Zondervan, 1994).

25. V. Raymond Edman, *But God* (Grand Rapids: Zondervan, 1962), 13.

26. J. Sidlow Baxter, *Awake, My Heart* (Grand Rapids: Zondervan, 1960), 103.

27. Joan Minninger, *Total Recall* (Emmaus, PA: Rodale Press, 1984), 3.

28. Hyman J. Appelman, *When the World Is on Fire* (Grand Rapids: Zondervan, 1962), from chapter 3, "All Out for Jesus Christ."

29. This story is told by Leslie B. Flynn in *Your Inner You* (Wheaton, IL: Victor Books, 1984), 60.

30. A. B. Kendall, "Confessing and Denying Christ" in *The Herald of Gospel Liberty* (July 17, 1919), 20.

31. René Pache, *The Inspiration and Authority of the Scripture* (Chicago: Moody Press, 1969), 45.

32. Arthur Flake, *Life at Eighty as I See It* (Nashville: Broadman Press, 1944), 97.

33 The definition of *meditation* as "memorizing, visualizing, and personalizing," and of *wisdom* as "seeing life from God's points of view" are from recollections of a Bill Gothard Seminar I attended in 1971. Those are phrases I remember Gothard using.

34. "A Primer on Meditation" is a nine-page booklet that is published by the Navigators. No author is given and no date is cited. The quotes are from pages 2, 4, and 5.

35. J. C. Ryle, *Five Christian Leaders of the 18th Century* (Guilford & London: Banner of Truth, 1960), 53.

36. "Start Young . . . Give Small Doses," *Family Life Today* (January 1975), 4.

37. Amy Carmichael, *Edges of His Ways* (Fort Washington, PA: Christian Literature Crusade, 1998), 41.

38. Arthur T. Pierson, *Many Infallible Proofs, Volume Two* (Grand Rapids: Zondervan, 2009), 111.

39. Quoted by Paul Lee Tan, *Encyclopedia of 7700 Illustrations* (Rockville, MD: Assurance Publishers, 1979), 511.

40. Amy Carmichael, *Edges of His Ways* (Fort Washington, PA: Christian Literature Crusade, 1998), 61.

41. S. D. Gordon, *Quiet Talks on Prayer* (Fleming H. Revell, 2010), 177, 182.

42. Samuel Rutherford, *Letters of Samuel Rutherford* (Edinburgh: Oliphant, Anderson, and Ferrier, 1891), 385.

43. *Converted and Called* (Nashville: The Gideons International), 101–2.

44. Herbert Lockyer, *All the Doctrines of the Bible* (Grand Rapids: Zondervan, 1964), 204.

45. Eric Betz, "He Found Inner Peace" (submitted by Jack Aynejian), *The Gideon* (March 2005), 3.

46. Thomas Chalmers, *Sermons by the Late Thomas Chalmers* (New York: Harper & Brothers, 1849), 43.

47. Randy Alcorn, *Heaven* (Wheaton: Tyndale House, 2004), 322.

48. Used by permission. I have previously related this story in my book, *He Shall Be Called* (New York: Warner Faith, 2005), 44.

49. Quoted by Al Bryant in *Climbing the Heights* (Grand Rapids: Zondervan, 1956), 21.

50. Solomon Ginsburg, *A Wandering Jew in Brazil* (Nashville: Sunday School Board of the Southern Baptist Convention, 1922), 19–20.

51. J. Sidlow Baxter, *The Master Theme of the Bible* (Wheaton, IL: Tyndale House Publishers, 1985), 180.

52. John MacArthur, *1 Corinthians* (Chicago: Moody Press, 1984), 398.

53. From various media accounts.

54. Vernon Whaley, *The Dynamics of Corporate Worship* (Grand Rapids: Baker, 2001), 60.

55. James C. Whittaker, *We Thought We Heard the Angels Sing* (NY: E. P. Dutton, 1943), 64.

56. Rosalind Goforth, *How I Know God Answers Prayer,* 1921.

57. From Charles Spurgeon's sermon, "A Present Religion," May 30, 1858.

58. These devotional thoughts are adapted from the author's book, *The Promise: How God Works All Things Together for Good* (Nashville; B&H Publishing Group, 2008).

59. Charles Haddon Spurgeon, *Beside Still Waters,* Roy H. Clark, ed. (Nashville: Thomas Nelson, 1999), 243.

60. John A. Broadus, "All Things Work Together for Good," in *Christian Herald,* Vol. 21, No. 35 (August 28, 1890).

61. Warren W. Wiersbe, *With the Word* (Nashville: Thomas Nelson, 1991), 517.

62. Bill Bright, *Discover the Book God Wrote* (Carol Stream, IL: Tyndale House, 2004), 177.

63. Virginia Law, *Appointment Congo* (Chicago: Rand McNally, 1966), 20–21.

64. "Ford Left Lasting Impressions on Colleagues in Michigan," in *The Michigan Daily,* December 13, 2006, at http://www.michigandaily.com/content/ford-left-lasting-impressions-colleagues-michigan, accessed December 27, 2006.

65. Hannah Hurnard, *Hinds' Feet on High Places* (Shippensburg, PA: Destiny Image Publishers, 1993), 197.

66. From a clipping in my files. Source of quote unknown.

67. Quoted by James Gilchrist Lawson in *Deeper Experiences of Famous Christians* (Anderson, IN: Warner Press, 1911), 190.

68 For the full story behind this hymn, see my book, *Then Sings My Soul* (Nashville: Thomas Nelson, 2004), 11.

69. This account is adapted from George Müller's book, *Answers to Prayer from George Müller's Narratives,* compiled by A. E. C. Brooks (Chicago: Moody Press, 2007), 37–39. As a further note, this small prayer group in Ireland just happened to begin at the same time—the same week—as a prayer meeting that began on Fulton Street in New York City that led to a similar revival in the United States, known as the Fulton Street Revival—but that's another story.

70. Wesley Duewel, *Revival Fire* (Grand Rapids: Zondervan, 1995), 352.

71. Adapted from numerous sources including James and Marti Hefley, *By Their Blood* (Grand Rapids: Baker Book House), 586–87.

72. Adapted from Corrie Ten Boom, *Clippings from My Notebook* (Nashville: Thomas Nelson, 1982), 53–55.

73 Henry T. Blackaby and Richard Blackaby, *Experiencing God Day by Day* (Nashville: B&H Publishing Group, 2006), 279.

74. Clayborne Carson, ed., *The Autobiography of Martin Luther King, Jr.* (New York: Warner Books, 1998), 9.

75. James Montgomery Boice, *Whatever Happened to the Gospel of Grace?* (Wheaton, IL: Crossway Books, 2001), 60.

76. The quotes in this devotional are taken from J. C. Ryle, *Be Zealous* (Ipswich: Hunt & Son, 1852) and are condensed and slightly updated and edited.

77. From a clipping in my files. Source of quote unknown.

78. Richard Wurmbrand, *Tortured for Christ* (Bartlesville, OK: Living Sacrifice Book Company, 1967), 45.

79. Charles Haddon Spurgeon, *John Ploughman's Talks* (New York: Sheldon & Company), 139.

80. Vance Havner, *In Times like These* (Old Tappan, NJ: Fleming H. Revell, 1969), 73.

81. A. W. Tozer, *Whatever Happened to Worship* (Camp Hill, PA: Christian Publications, 1985), 30–31.

82. Vance Havner, *The Secret of Christian Joy* (Old Tappan, New Jersey, 1938), 40.

83. Adapted from "A Father's Influence," by Robert Webber in *What My Parents Did Right,* compiled and edited by Gloria Gaither (Nashville: Star Song Publishing Group, 1991), 207–8.

84. Joseph Parker, *Joseph Parker's People's Bible*, Vol. 13: Proverbs (New York: Funk & Wagnalls, 1891), 197.

85. René Pache, *The Person and Work of the Holy Spirit* (Chicago: Moody Press, 1979, paperback edition), 119.

86. Andrew Murray, *Humility and Absolute Surrender* (Peabody, MA: Hendrickson Christian Classics, 2005), 27.

87. Quoted by Warren W. Wiersbe in *With the Word Bible Commentary* (Nashville: Thomas Nelson, 1991), comment on Galatians 5.

88. F. B. Boreham, *Shadows on the Wall* (New York: Abingdon Press, 1922), 68–70.

89. Al Bryant, comp., *Climbing the Heights* (Grand Rapids: Zondervan, 1956), 231.

90. William Dobbie, *A Very Present Help* (Chicago: Moody Press, 1945), 11.

91. E. A. Johnston, *J. Sidlow Baxter: A Heart Awake* (Grand Rapids: Baker Books, 2005), 124–26.

92. Ruth Bell Graham, *It's My Turn* (Old Tappan, NJ: Fleming H. Revell Company, 1982), 136–37.

93. John R. Rice, *God's Cure for Anxious Care* (Murfreesboro, TN: Sword of the Lord Publishers, 1973), 12–13.

94. Martyn Lloyd-Jones, *Spiritual Depression: Its Causes and Cure* (Grand Rapids: Eerdmans, 1965), 271–72.

95. I. D. E. Thomas, comp., *A Puritan Golden Treasury,* (Carlisle, PA: Banner of Truth, 2000), 206.

96. Joy Ridderhof, *Are You Rejoicing* (Los Angeles: Gospel Recordings, 1984), entry for day 18.

97. William Gresley, *Sermons Preached at Brighton* (London: Joseph Masters, 1853), 195.

98. This is from Charles Haddon Spurgeon's sermon, "All Joy in All Trials," preached on February 4, 1883. I've made slight editorial changes to condense and update the quoted portion.

99. J. I. Packer, *Knowing God* (Downers Grove, IL: InterVarsity Press, 1973), 225.

100. Joseph Parker, *The People's Bible: Vol. XIII, the Proverbs* (New York: Funk & Wagnalls, 1891), 317.

101. Clarence W. Hall, *Samuel Logan Brengle: Portrait of a Prophet* (Atlanta: The Salvation Army Supplies and Purchasing Dept., 1933), 247.

102. Hannah Whitall Smith, *Living in the Sunshine* (New York: Fleming H. Revell, 1906), 160–61, 163.

103. Alexander Maclaren, *Expositions of Holy Scripture,* in his sermon on this verse.

104. John R. Rice, comp., *The Best of Billy Sunday* (Murfreesboro, TN: Sword of the Lord, 1965), 240.

105. Andrew Murray, *With Christ in the School of Prayer* (Old Tappan, NJ: Fleming H. Revell, 1953), 229.

106. Ibid.

107. This synopsis and these quotes are from Dr. Robert A. Emmons, *Thanks! How Practicing Gratitude Can Make You Happier* (Boston: Houghton Mifflin Company, 2008), from chapter 1: "The New Science of Gratitude."

108. In a personal conversation with the author.

109. Adapted from the author's book, *From This Verse* (Nashville: Thomas Nelson, 1998), entry for November 8. Spurgeon related this story in his sermon "All of Grace."

110. Ibid.

111. Adapted from the author's book, *From This Verse* (Nashville: Thomas Nelson, 1998), entry for November 9.

112. I. D. E. Thomas, comp., *A Puritan Golden Treasury* (Carlisle, PA: Banner of Truth, 2000), 121.

113. Paul Maier in the foreword of *How Christianity Changed the World* by Alvin J. Schmidt (Grand Rapids: Zondervan Publishing House, 2001, 2004), 8–9.

114. From Martin Luther's sermon on Galatians 4:1–7.

115. In the *Holman Christian Standard Bible*, the words, "I have been crucified with Christ" appear in verse 19.

116. Some of the material for Galatians 2:20 previously appeared in the author's book, *My All in All* (Nashville: B&H Publishing Group, 2008), installment for April 25.

117. *Bible Knowledge Commentary/New Testament*, ed. John F. Walvoord and Roy B. Zuck (Colorado Springs: Victor, 2000), 682.

118. Frederick W. Robertson, *Sermons Preached at Brighton* (New York: Harper & Brothers, 1899), 529.

119. J. I. Packer, *Knowing God* (Downers Grove, IL: InterVarsity Press, 1973), 18.

120. The thoughts on this page are adapted from the author's book, *My All in All* (Nashville: B&H Publishing Group, 2008), entries for July 21 and October 25.

121. This quote is frequently attributed to Mother Teresa, but I'm unaware of the original source.

122. Hyman Appelman, *When the Word is on Fire* (Grand Rapids: Zondervan, 1962), from chapter 3, "All Out for Jesus Christ."

123. Martin Luther, *Lectures on Romans*, ed. Wilhelm Pauck (Louisville, KY: Westminster John Knox, 1961), 18.

124. Dana Thompson in personal interviews with Rob Morgan and Sherry Anderson, September 21–22, 2009, used with permission.

125. Quoted in Spurgeon's *Treasury of David,* in the commentary for Psalm 56, publ, date.

126. In *Treasury of David,* note on Psalm 4:8.

127. Charles Henry Mackintosh, *Notes on the Book of Exodus* (New York: Loizeaux Brothers, 1880), 186.

128. David Livingstone, *Missionary Travels and Researches in South Africa* (New York: Harper & Brothers, 1872), 626.

129. Rosalind Goforth, *How I Know God Answers Prayer: The Personal Testimony of One Lifetime,* published in 1921.

130. A. W. Tozer, *A Treasury of A. W. Tozer* (Grand Rapids: Baker, 1980), 58.

131. Ibid., 57.

132. J. Wilber Chapman, *The Secret of a Happy Day* (Grand Rapids: Baker Book House, 1979, based on an 1899 edition), ix.

133. William Evans, *The Shepherd Psalm* (Chicago: The Bible Institute Colportage Association, 1921), 27.

134. F. B. Meyer, *The Shepherd Psalm* (New Canaan, CT: Keats Publishing, 1984), 149.

135. Thomas Watson, *Gleanings from Thomas Watson* (Morgan, PA: Soli Deo Gloria Publications, 1995), 86.

136. We don't know whether this message was spoken, sung, or both, but it's traditional to think of the angels singing it.

137. Dietrich Bonhoeffer, *I Want to Live These Days with You: A Year of Daily Devotions* (Louisville, KY: Westminster John Knox Press, 2007), 375.

138. This is my own composition, but it's based on similar pieces of writings I've heard or read through the years.

139. Edward Osborne, *The Children's Savior* (London: Rivingtons Waterloo Place, 1882), 4.

140. R. A. Torrey, *The Return of the Lord Jesus* (Los Angeles: The Bible Institute of Los Angeles, 1913), 38.

141. Daniel Gilbert, *Stumbling on Happiness* (New York: Knoph Doubleday Publishing Group, 2007), 17.

142. Randy Alcorn, *Heaven* (Carol Stream, IL: Tyndale House Publishers, 2004), 158–59.

143. Richard Leonard and JoNancy Linn Sundberg, comp., *A Glimpse of Heaven* (New York: Howard Books, 2007), 159.

144. A. J. Gordon, *Ecce Venit* (New York: F. H. Revell, 1889), 213.

145. *New Bible Commentary: 21st Century Edition* (Downers Grove, IL: Intervarsity Press, 1994), comment on Revelation 22:20.

STEPS TO PEACE WITH GOD

1. RECOGNIZE GOD'S PLAN—PEACE AND LIFE

The message in this book stresses that God loves you and wants you to experience His peace and life.

The BIBLE says ... For God loved the world so much that He gave His only Son, so that everyone who believes in Him may not die but have eternal life. John 3:16

2. REALIZE OUR PROBLEM—SEPARATION FROM GOD

People choose to disobey God and go their own way. This results in separation from God.

The BIBLE says ... Everyone has sinned and is far away from God's saving presence. Romans 3:23

3. RESPOND TO GOD'S REMEDY—THE CROSS OF CHRIST

God sent His Son to bridge the gap. Christ did this by paying the penalty of our sins when He died on the cross and rose from the grave.

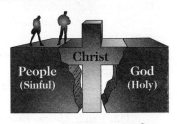

The BIBLE says ... But God has shown us how much He loves us—it was while we were still sinners that Christ died for us! Romans 5:8

4. RECEIVE GOD'S SON—LORD AND SAVIOR

You cross the bridge into God's family when you ask Christ to come into your life.

The BIBLE says ... Some, however, did receive Him and believed in Him; so He gave them the right to become God's children. John 1:12

THE INVITATION IS TO:
REPENT (turn from your sins), ASK for God's forgiveness, and by faith RECEIVE Jesus Christ into your heart and life and follow Him in obedience as your Lord and Savior.

PRAYER OF COMMITMENT
"Dear Lord Jesus, I know that I am a sinner, and I ask for Your forgiveness. I believe You died for my sins and rose from the dead. I turn from my sins and invite You to come into my heart and life. I want to trust and follow You as my Lord and Savior. In Your Name, Amen."

If you are committing your life to Christ, please let us know!

Billy Graham Evangelistic Association
1 Billy Graham Parkway, Charlotte, NC 28201-0001
1-877-2GRAHAM (1-877-247-2426)
billygraham.org/Commitment

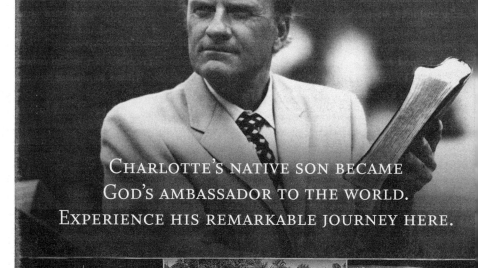

CHARLOTTE'S NATIVE SON BECAME
GOD'S AMBASSADOR TO THE WORLD.
EXPERIENCE HIS REMARKABLE JOURNEY HERE.

Visit the Billy Graham Library in Charlotte and retrace the amazing story of one of America's most well-known pastors. Explore historical re-creations, multimedia exhibits, galleries of memorabilia, plus exciting updates including Billy Graham's personal collection of books. Tour the Graham family homeplace, browse unique gifts, or relax over lunch in our café. No matter how you spend your time here, you'll discover an experience that is

TOTALLY INSPIRING.

FREE

The BILLY GRAHAM Library

MON —TO— SAT 9³⁰-5

704-401-3200

BILLYGRAHAMLIBRARY.ORG

Reservations required for groups of 15 or more; call 704-401-3270 or email librarytours@bgea.org.
4330 Westmont Drive (just off Billy Graham Parkway), Charlotte, NC 28217

©2011 BGEA · A ministry of Billy Graham Evangelistic Association

Come Away...

Come away to the Blue Ridge
Mountains near Asheville, N.C.,
and hear God speak through
inspiring teachers, soul-stirring
worship, and the breathtaking
beauty of His creation.
For a free program guide,
call 1-800-950-2092 or visit
TheCove.org.

BILLY
GRAHAM
Training Center *at* The Cove

A ministry of Billy Graham Evangelistic Association

©2011 BGEA